The Complete Guide to Passive Diversified Real Estate Investing

*How to achieve your retirement
and financial goals without
the headaches of being a landlord!*

by
Lon Welsh
Author of *The Colorado Guide to Real Estate Investing*

For information to reproduce selections from this book, write to:

Permissions
Ironton Capital Management, LLC
2755 S. Locust Street, #150
Denver, CO 80222

First Edition

Library of Congress Cataloguing-in-Publication Data

ISBN 979-8-9907749-0-2

9798990774902

"If you are an active real estate investor, a person looking for a 'better way' to retirement, or someone who needs to diversify your investments... this book is for you!

"Lon's expertise in passive investing is outstanding and I highly recommend this book for anyone looking to improve their financial future." ~ Joe Massey, Senior Loan Officer, Castle & Cooke Mortgage

"In 2006 I discovered Lon's Brokerage that emphasized real estate investing. In 2012 I joined his Brokerage to learn more regarding real estate investment. I made my first real estate investment in 2016.

"Prior to that I was in the industry 26 years and never bought an investment property. Have you ever heard of paralysis of fear? That was me when it came to investing.

"Now, I'm at the point where I'm wondering how to become involved in passive real estate investing. Fortunately, this time I don't intend to wait 26 years!

"I have found this to be the perfect book to learn more about being passive or diversifying in real estate investing. I've gained a good foundation of what type of real estate investments opportunities exist, how to approach these opportunities, what is the time and financial commitment, which opportunity to choose for my personality and retirement goals. There's even a flow chart that's helping me decide which path to take.

"If you ever wanted to invest actively or passively and didn't know where to start. This book is a very good source to have on hand to guide you. " ~ Bill Fung, HomeSell Inc. President

What Our Investors Say

"Yes! Ironton Capital has helped me by reducing the time and headaches I had when I managed my residential rentals. Ironton Capital is on track to beat the returns that my rentals were generating in the current economic conditions. Thank you, Lon and Team!" ~ Jay S.

"After working with Lon for many years, I've found his approach very thoughtful, analytical, and deliberate. He invests based on principals and a proven methodology with a very unique approach to identifying and underwriting investment opportunities based on historical analysis and proven modeling techniques." ~ Jesse K.

"Before Ironton, the performance of my retirement assets had been inconsistent at best even under professional management. I believe I have moved my money from an unpredictable market subject to many economic factors and significant risk, to a fundamentally sound business model that is a hedge against inflation. I have confidence in the leadership/management team at Ironton and would recommend their funds to family and friends with confidence." ~ John S.

"We all know that interpreting current market conditions and determining where to invest is incredibly challenging in this environment right now. I have always been ready to invest in Ironton Capital funds. Lon has a freakish ability to understand and analyze real estate deals. He has surrounded himself with a great team of like-minded experienced investors that know where and when to direct funds for maximum gain." ~ Tom M.

"In the last 15 months, I had 4 tenants non renew their leases and worked on rental properties non-stop. Although I still am an active investor, I've significantly reduced the amount of work by selling many of our rentals and investing passively with Ironton Capital. It feels good to have time back with the now passive investments. Ironton made it really easy." ~ Jared C.

"I had set a goal years ago of how much I wanted to generate in passive income from equity produced by my hard work as the owner of a small business for 13 years. Based on the projected returns on the National Diversified Funds as well as periodic cash flows generated by the Short Term and Medium Term Funds, I've been able to establish a profile of investments that is anticipated to outperform my original goals. This relationship has allowed me to move from active to passive income." ~ Justin H.

"Ironton Capital provides us access to a geographically and sector diverse real estate portfolio that is carefully curated given well-defined investment parameters, targeted sub-markets and established development partners. Relative to other bespoke, privately offered real estate funds, the structure, transparency and modest approach of National Diversified Fund is well-suited for investors that have the capital to put at risk but are perhaps newer to the investment class." ~ Heidi W.

"I chose to invest with Ironton Capital because their track record of making sound, responsible investment decisions gave me the confidence and conviction to invest. It is clear they have the knowledge and expertise to make informed, strategic decisions with my capital, while also prioritizing safety and responsibility." ~ Shalom K.

"My primary focus is on the process of moving to growing my family's net worth to passive income and having our operating business run on its own and pay me a nice salary. Lon brings a scientific approach and financial sophistication to this process that is at a very high level. I personally have more confidence in Lon's abilities to create a strong return for my family than anyone else. Importantly, Lon is currently able to source strong deals that others are having a hard time sourcing. Lon also helped me assess under what circumstances I am better off selling on 1031 or paying tax and putting into other investments. This has been a key part of our wealth planning." ~ Jason B.

About the Author

Lon Welsh founded Your Castle Real Estate, the largest independent brokerage in Colorado, with over 700 Realtors and 4,800+ transactions ($2.5 billion) in 2022. He co-founded First Alliance Title, a Colorado top ten title company. A former strategic consultant with Deloitte, then Arthur Andersen (Accenture) for eight years, he has been a landlord for over 20 years, peaking at over 140 residential rentals. He then sold most of the residential to purchase commercial buildings.

He's also been teaching investors for over 20 years on how to thrive with real estate investing. Lon has written over a dozen books including *The Colorado Guide to Real Estate Investing* and has created a lot of millionaires over that time. Yet he found that for every one person who would act to buy a rental to actively invest, that nineteen would not because they just didn't have the time.

For those 95% of the people that want quality, investment-grade real estate in their portfolio but don't want to be an active investor, he founded Ironton Capital in 2019. Lon assembled a passionate team with diverse expertise in accounting, banking, and investing with the goal to create over $100 million of wealth for IC investors over the next decade while building up their local communities.

As of the time of this writing, Ironton Capital works with 300+ clients, managing $70+ million in assets. Their growth funds historically have returned over 17% IRR per year. Their liquid income funds historically generate 8-12% annually.

While investing is Lon's passion, he has always found that true fulfillment comes from the familial bond with his team and fostering growth in the real estate community. Lon is a father of 3, pursues travel, wine, golf, tennis, running, and skiing in his free time. He serves on the boards and investment committees of the Denver Zoo, the Denver/Aurora Ronald McDonald House, and Denver Boys and Girls Club.

Also by the Author

Thrive: How Realtors Can Succeed in Any Market, 2024
Lon Welsh, Rick Davidson, Eric Flohr

Unlocked: Revealing the Eight Secrets of Highly Efficient Sales Professionals
Darice Johnston, Lon Welsh, Bruce Gardner, Drew Shope

The Real Estate IRA Retirement Planning Guide
Jeff Sibel, with Lon Welsh and Charles Roberts

The Practical Guide to Colorado Real Estate Investing (2018)
Lon Welsh, Charles Roberts, Greg Parham, Joe Massey

The Practical Guide to Colorado Real Estate Investing (2016)
Lon Welsh, Charles Roberts, Greg Parham, Joe Massey

Game Changers, 2014
Steve Murray, Lorne Wallace, Lon Welsh

The 2013 Guide to Colorado Real Estate Investing
Lon Welsh, Charles Roberts, Jon Roberts, Tony Girard, John
Dovenbarger, Greg Parham

How to Thrive with Social Media and Blogging, 2011
Kris Andrea, Steve Depperschmidt, LaTonia Gore, Greg Parham,
Lon Welsh

The 2011 Guide to Colorado Real Estate Investing
Lon Welsh, Charles Roberts, Ben Dorland, Jon Sommer, Tony
Girard

Thrive: How Realtors Can Succeed in a Down Market, 2010
Lon Welsh, Bruce Gardner, Mike Welk, Drew Shope

The 2009 Guide to Denver Real Estate Investing
Lon Welsh, Charles Roberts, Michael Canon, Mike Welk

Contents

Acknowledgements

Sir Isaac Newton, the famous English scientist, once said, "If I have seen further, it is by standing on the shoulders of giants."

After over twenty years of working in investment real estate, I owe a debt to literally hundreds of people. I learned the most from the investor-focused Realtors at Your Castle Real Estate. I could not have figured all of this out on my own.

Introduction

Why I Wrote this Book

I have written many books, taught hundreds of classes, and thousands of investors how to actively invest in real estate. Most of my students learned that real estate investing could be a key addition to their financial plan. (I'll show you the numbers later in this chapter.)

However, what I found is that less than 5% of the people that came to my classes went on to buy a property as an active investor. When I asked them why, it wasn't because they didn't believe in real estate. They were just too busy with their professional jobs and their family life. Others thought the hassle factor of being an active investor – even with a property manager – was not appealing.

What this taught me is that for each one active real estate investor, there are about twenty families that are better suited for passive real estate investing for their financial plans. This book is for you.

I also found many active investors who, like me, were fed up with the hassles of being a landlord. They wanted to transition to passive investing while retaining their tax advantages. This book is for you too!

Who Should Read This Book

Have you ever wondered if you could reap the benefits of real estate investing without the hefty time investment as well? If you could participate in commercial grade investments without having to write a million-dollar check? If passive real estate investing is a realistic option for your financial freedom? This book is designed to help you answer these questions.

Regrettably, this option is not open to everyone. To participate in private equity investments, the Securities and Exchange Commission (SEC) requires you to be an accredited investor to take advantage of these type of investment opportunities.

That's someone who meets any one of these criteria:

- Individual, with an income over $200,000 in the last 2 years.
- Household (with spouse or partner), with an income over $300,000 in the last 2 years.
- Has investable assets of $1,000,000 or more, not including your primary residence (individually or with spouse or partner).

This roughly equates to the top five percent of all US households.

As of the time of this writing, June 2024, Congress is considering loosening the standards for an accredited investor, so if you do not yet meet this requirement but are working towards it, this book will help you prepare for that time so you can start investing with confidence, and with the aid of your financial advisors, as soon as you become accredited.

Important Legal Disclaimers

- I'm not a CPA or an attorney. You will want to have your financial professionals help you develop your plan.
- Ironton Capital is not a financial or investment advisor. We do not promise or guarantee any income or particular result from your use of the information. Your use of the information contained herein is at your own risk.
- The funds discussed in this book are for illustrative purposes only. None of this material should be construed as an offer to invest.

If you find what we share here interesting, we can provide you with the subscription documents. You'll want to have your attorney and CPA help you review them.

Typical Financial Goals

Have you ever sat down to plan your financial future and wondered:

1. Will I have enough for retirement?
2. Can I retire comfortably before I'm too old to enjoy it?
3. Will I be able to… send a child or grandchild to college, own a family vacation home, leave a legacy for my family, or give back to my community?

Then you pulled out your computer and checked out Oppenheimer, Fidelity, Vanguard or a similar web site. You were probably told that your current rate of savings, combined with typical stock market returns, will not enable you to meet your goals. <u>You needed to find another way</u>.

Retirement worries are common among Americans, with a notable percentage expressing concerns about their financial readiness for later years. The Employee Benefit Research Institute's 2021 survey revealed that 4 in 10 American workers are projected to fall short of what they need in retirement savings. This finding underscores the widespread nature of retirement anxieties, cutting across various demographics.

The Pew Research Center's study highlighted the generational aspect of these concerns, with 61% of young adults, 64% of middle-aged adults, and 57% of older adults expressing worry about their retirement savings.

You've likely discovered that real estate is likely part of the solution to your financial objectives. It will diversify your investments from just stocks and bonds and historically it generates much higher returns.

But you are likely a busy professional, with an even busier partner. Whatever limited free time you do have, you don't want to spend running real estate investments. Isn't there a way to do invest passively with a managed amount of risk?

That's what we're here to investigate together!

Retirement Calculator – Stocks/Bonds Plan

Briefly, let's determine how much you can withdraw from your retirement savings annually while ensuring it lasts your lifetime. This depends on various factors, including your age, life expectancy, investment returns, and spending habits. You'll want to work with your CPA or financial planner to develop a more robust estimate than the quick estimate here, but this should give you a rough idea.

A common rule of thumb is the 4% rule, which suggests withdrawing 4% of your retirement savings in the first year and adjusting for inflation thereafter.

For example, if you have $500,000 saved, you could withdraw $20,000 in the first year. This rule aims to balance spending needs with the preservation of savings.

In other words, to get $1 of consistent retirement income, you need $25 in savings. The formula is:

$1 spending / 4% return = $25 in savings

If you want $200,000 of annual income in retirement:

$200,000 annual spend / 4% return = $5,000,000 in savings

No wonder so many people are stressed about retirement savings! Vanguard reports that over the last 70 years, a typical 60% stock and 40% bond portfolio has generated an average annual return of approximately 7% to 8%. Actual returns can vary depending on specific market conditions and investment strategies employed within the portfolio.

And over the past 70 years, the average US rate of inflation has been about 3% per year. This figure reflects the general increase in prices for goods and services over an extended period, as measured by indices such as the Consumer Price Index (CPI).

The 4% withdraw rule is just the expected return (7%) less the expected inflation (3%). The amount you can draw out of savings each year will grow a bit, to keep pace with inflation.

7% total return – 3% expected inflation =
4% annual withdraw amount

Retirement Calculator – Real Estate Plan

If you want a better retirement lifestyle, you need to increase the return from 7-8% to something higher, without taking a lot of extra risk – and that's why a lot of us turn to real estate.

A well-diversified real portfolio of 30-40 commercial properties can generate a return of 17-20% per year. Assume 17% and take 3% off for the inflation factor. That leaves 14%.

How does this impact your savings requirement?

$200,000 annual spend / 14% return = $1,430,000 in savings

You have reduced your savings requirement from $5,000,000 to $1,430,000, and still achieved the same $200,000 annual spend goal. And there are advantages to the risk adverse. A well-diversified real estate portfolio typically exhibits lower investment return risk compared to a stock and bond portfolio.

Real estate returns are notably less volatile than the average annual return of U.S. stocks, as reported by data from the Credit Suisse Global Investment Returns Yearbook. While real estate values can fluctuate, they generally don't experience the same level of short-term price swings as stocks.

In fact, according to research by the National Council of Real Estate Investment Fiduciaries (NCREIF), real estate investments often provide more stable and predictable returns over the long term, with less volatility than stocks.

What's the drawback? Liquidity.

It's essential to note that **real estate investments are much less liquid than stocks and bonds**, meaning they can be harder to sell quickly if needed. **You wouldn't want ALL your portfolio to be in real estate for this reason**. You've got to be diversified.

Retirement Calculator – Diversified Plan

Overall, a diversified portfolio including both real estate and stocks/bonds can help mitigate overall investment risk while potentially enhancing returns.

For example, if you put half of your savings into diversified real estate and half into a traditional stock/bond portfolio, you'd expect a return about halfway between 7-8% (stocks/bonds) and 17-20% (real estate), or 13%. Take out 3% for inflation. How much savings do we need now?

$200,000 annual spend / 10% return = $2,000,000 in savings
For most Americans, saving $2,000,000 for retirement is a lot more realistic than saving $5,000,000. You can retire sooner and retire better by adding real estate for diversification.

Active or Passive Real Estate?

Now that you understand that you need some real estate in your portfolio, should you invest in active or passive real estate?

You may have had a life-long dream to own and/or operate a real estate investment. While diving into active investing is outside the scope of this book, I have included the first chapter of my active investing book in the appendix. You can go through the worksheets and see for yourself what it would take to engage in active real estate investing with confidence.

The appendix will give you an overview of:

- The major types of active real estate investments, like fix and flips or small residential rentals.
- The dimensions of what is needed to be successful, including:
  o Credit scores
  o Cash available to invest
  o Risk tolerance of you and your spouse/partner
  o Skill and desire to work with construction contractors and more

- A detailed analysis of what it takes to be successful with each category of active investment. I had a front row seat for over twenty years to watch hundreds of investors try their hand at active investment as well as digging in myself. I can help you save a lot of time by sharing our lessons with you!
- A detailed flow chart to determine which active investment categories are most appropriate and likely to succeed given your current profile of interests and resources.

If this sounds interesting to you, have a look later. You may find that active investment is a great match for where you are now.

However, while you may find active investing interesting, if you are reading this book, then you are likely extremely busy, and this may not be the best time for your family to start the active investing journey.

Or you might find it just is not that appealing once you know the truth about what it takes to stack the odds in your favor. It's harder than it looks and it's a steep learning curve. In fact, it takes just as much time and effort to master active investing as your current career!

If that is the case, passive real estate investing may be right for you. The mission of this book is to help you assess that for yourself.

Building and running the largest independent real estate brokerage in Colorado, we completed thousands of deals each year and many of those were for investors. I had a front row seat to see what worked and what didn't. Yet, with all my contacts and experience, I still could not find any simple, comprehensive reference guide to provide an orientation on passive investing and how to make the switch from active to passive.

My goal in this book is to help a potential investor, with no prior experience, understand the basics of passive real estate investing, so you can decide if passive investing is right for you.

If you are already an active investor, then my goal is to help you make the transition to passive investor while retaining your tax advantages.

We will start by walking through common mistakes I have seen investors make over the years. I'll provide some real-world examples to bring these to life and share some success stories, and some failures too, so you can learn from our triumphs and mistakes!

By the end of this short guide, you'll have the confidence to know what questions you should ask as you start to evaluate investments and build your own passive portfolio.

Chapter 1: Paths to Investing

How I got Involved in Passive Investing

I've been an active real estate investor for over twenty years. I first got interested in real estate when I was trying to figure out my own retirement plan in my late twenties.

As shown above, the Vanguard web site I visited suggested you could spend 4% of your portfolio a year when you retire. If you want a $200,000 retirement income, you'd need a stock and bond portfolio of $5 million. My wife and I both had great jobs, but that seemed like a lot to have to save up in our 401k and IRAs!

We needed to find another way. I started to learn about real estate investing as an alternative. I really liked what I found.

In the mid-1990's, it was plausible that you could make 20% annualized IRR (internal rate of return) with real estate. The IRR is a metric that captures all four ways in which real estate generates wealth:

- Cashflow from the tenant each month.
- Paying down the principal of the loan.
- Tax benefits, such as writing off depreciation to reduce your current income tax.
- Appreciation.

By comparison, the stock market over the last 50 years has generated around 10% IRR. The bond market returns quite a bit less than that.

Albert Einstein once said that compounding interest is the eighth wonder of the world. See for yourself:

	Real Estate	Stocks	Bonds
Initial Investment	$100,000	$100,000	$100,000
Annualized IRR	20%	10%	5.5%
Value in 5 years	$248,832	$161,051	$130,696
Value in 10 years	$619,174	$259,374	$170,814
Value in 20 years	$3,833,760	$672,750	$291,776

We saw it too, so my wife and I decided real estate was for us. In 1998 when we moved to Denver, we bought a bungalow in Washington Park, a neighborhood just south of downtown Denver, for $219,000 (it would be worth over $800K today with compounding interest!) We put in a separate entrance and created a basement apartment unit that we rented out. It made a big dent in the mortgage. The key skill here was networking to find different tradespeople to help me with the work. It wasn't too hard to build out, and it was very easy to rent.

I wish I could still find deals like this on the Multiple Listing Service (MLS)!!! I bought several more rental buildings after that.

Real Estate Fix and Flips

We started doing fix and flips (F&F) in 2000 to generate more cashflow. In the late 1990's and early 2000's, the average DOM (days on market) was 80-90 days. There was lots of inventory to look at. It wasn't too hard to find good projects. The best projects would get 2-3 offers and sell in a week, but most "average" deals were on the market for at least a month, and you were the only buyer. The key skill for F&F is to have a good vision for what a successful remodel will look like, and not do too much. It's important that the style of your work is consistent with the neighborhood and architecture of the building.

For my F&F, I restored a huge Washington Park Victorian that had been carved into a triplex. Some of my contractors turned out to be crooks. It was a LOT of work, and some of the more modern finishes we picked – at that time – were not desired by buyers in that neighborhood. It took twice as long as I expected and certainly went over budget. I got a decent amount of negative feedback about my finish selections. We eventually sold it for about half of the profit expected. That was sweat equity!

I learned a lot. My next project was much smaller and had a highly focused scope of work. I got a lot more precise in screening contractors. We finished a full remodel in six weeks vs fourteen. Again, a Victorian, but this time we got the finishes the market wanted. Despite the average Days on Market (DOM) being near 90 days, we sold the house the first weekend for asking price. That was a highly profitable project. I was on my way.

Of my first eight F&Fs, I made money on seven and lost around $10K on one. It had a terrible floor plan. It was in a nice Denver area (Congress Park) on a beautiful block. But it had the worst floorplan, and there wasn't any good way to fix it. I thought a nice renovation in a great area would overcome the limitation of a poor plan. Nope. Couldn't sell it. Eventually gave it away. Never do a F&F if you can't figure out how to solve all the problems.

Doing a F&F is a big hobby/job if you want to make money from it. It is NOT passive. If I was running two at a time, it'd easily take me 30 hours a week, which was hard to do with a full-time job. Looking at properties, examining comps to determine what level of renovations to do, getting the loans, buying the homes, interviewing contractors and getting bids, supervising their work, solving lots of problems, then finally selling… geez it's a lot of work.

Value-Add Renovations

Next, I switched from F&F to buying to buying beat-up rentals. I could take a fourplex in disrepair with low rents (and/or high vacancy), repair the units, and re-lease at higher rents. With better cashflow, I could refinance the property, take out all my cash, and keep the asset.

You don't need a calculator to know that the IRR on this style of project will be VERY high. That kept me busy from 2002 to 2007. This time I used a property manager and hired a bookkeeper. I was starting to have a set of contractors I could (mostly) trust, so project management was less cumbersome. Since I held the asset for more than a year, when I did sell, it would qualify for capital gains tax vs. ordinary income, cutting my tax bill dramatically. Alternatively, I could do a 1031 exchange and defer my taxes. That was not an option with F&Fs (you need to own the asset for a year to qualify for a 1031 exchange, and most F&F should be completed in 3-6 months). I made less money, but it was so worth it to get my time back.

2008 wasn't a good year to buy, since the market fell an average of 25% in Denver. In nicer areas like the Highlands, prices didn't drop, or they only dropped a small amount. In lower priced neighborhoods, the values dropped 60-70%. It became clear by 2009 that we were at/near the bottom. Every homeowner that was foreclosed on became a tenant the next morning, so there was a lot of new demand for rentals.

One of the other members of the investment committee at Ironton Capital is Brent Guyor. He has a background as a CPA at KPMG and a real estate developer at Intrawest. He and I got the financial statements for most of the condo HOAs in Denver. We analyzed which were the strongest and built a priority list.

We started to buy many condos. In 2009, I had a memorably great deal where I bought a package of four 1BR and four 2BR condos in a nice complex for $340,000.

2009	# of Units	Price	Total Value
1 Bedroom Condo	4	$37,000	$148,000
2 Bedroom Condo	4	$48,000	$192,000
Total Value			$340,000
Downpayment		25%	$85,000
Mortgages			$255,000

They increased 500%+ in value by 2019.

2019	# of Units	Price	Total Value	Price 2019 versus 2009
1 Bedroom Condo	4	$190,000	$760,000	5.1
2 Bedroom Condo	4	$225,000	$900,000	4.7
Total Value			$1,660,000	4.9

My 25% downpayment increased in value by nearly 15x in ten years. I had great cash flow and easily paid off the mortgages in under ten years.

Total Value		$1,660,000
Sales Costs	5%	$83,000
Net Proceeds		$1,557,000
Gross Profit		$1,237,000
Initial Investment		$85,000
ROI		14.6

I wound up buying over eighty condos and townhomes in 2009-2012. Brent bought quite a few and we helped clients buy them by the dozens. I think it's highly unlikely that we'll ever see another opportunity THIS good. But there are always other opportunities in the future.

Working on bigger projects

Three or four years after buying all these cats and dogs, it was time to refinance and pull out a lot of equity. I used it to buy projects like a 30-unit apartment complex that had 30% vacancy with rents 25% below market. I did light renovations on the units, re-leased at market with a strong property manager, and fixed the utility issues (e.g., install LED lighting, low flow water fixtures, high efficiency laundry equipment, xeriscaping). The skills for this project were:

- Developing a good work plan and budget
- Being able to communicate effectively to a bank to get a loan on favorable terms
- Solving any problems that came up

2015-17 was about the end of when it was relatively easy to find apartment value-add projects like this. Too many people caught on to it. It became insanely competitive to find such projects.

I even tried building over 25 townhomes and spec homes. I discovered that I was making around a 20% IRR, which is fine. But real estate development doesn't have the same favorable tax treatment that apartment value-add has. And there is, in my view, a LOT more risk in development. Also, I found development work a lot more time-consuming and stressful. I'm sure there are new construction developers that would disagree with me – and I'm glad for that. It's a corner of the real estate market that isn't for me, and I'm glad it works for them!

By 2017 I started selling my properties off. In the past when I did this, I would use a 1031 tax-deferred exchange to find a bigger project. Since I was not able to find suitable projects with high enough returns, I just paid the capital gains tax. By that point, I had been a VERY active investor for twenty years and liked the idea of working less and skiing, golfing, and playing more tennis with my family. I started to research if passive real estate investing could be a viable option. The more I researched it, the more I liked it.

With active investing, I was responsible for (the short list):
1. Understanding the market trends.
2. Making intelligent purchase decisions about what sort of asset to buy, and how much (if any) renovation to do.
3. Finding the deal (which became increasingly difficult).
4. Running all the appropriate due diligence.
5. Arranging the financing, and personally being responsible for the loan.
6. While the property manager did most of the day to day, I still had to supervise the manager, as well as the bookkeeper.

There are enough problems to solve for everyone! While you own the project, you never really get out of the trenches. Then I had to decide when and how to sell at the right time…and manage the sales and negotiation process. Then be on a tight 1031 exchange close to repeat the process. (See the Appendix for the complete active investing checklists!)

It's the ultimate first world problem, and I'm sure plenty of readers would love to trade places with me…but it does feel like being on a treadmill, right?

Upgrading to Passive Investing

Therefore, I decided it was time to try life off the active investing treadmill. Instead of ME doing all the work, with passive investing, the project Sponsor does all that work.

The passive investor (the "limited partner" or LP) just sends in a check and cashes a check at the end. The LP usually gets a preferred return (often 5-8% per year), which means that they get paid first. But that was still a lot of work, participating in each project individually, and I had to write a large check for each investment, which was higher risk than I wanted to tolerate.

Then I discovered a third way. Rather than finding and negotiating with each Sponsor individually, there could be a General Partner (GP) who found multiple projects for the LPs and each LP could have a small piece of each project. The risk was mitigated, I could participate in more projects, and the GP could take care of all the due diligence and accounting for the LPs.

The LPs still get a preferred return and after the preferred return, GP and LPs share the profits in a "waterfall." The GP might get 20% of the profit and the LPs get 80%, up until a total of 20% annualized IRR has been paid. If there is any profit beyond that, the GP cut increases as an incentive to do well. I liked how everyone's interests are aligned and investing gets easier.

After a year of research into this fund of funds model, we made eight passive investments in 2019 to 2020. By early 2024 (about four years later), five investments had been completed and were paid off. The other three projects needed more time and should be completed in seven years (2026). We're on track for these initial eight investments to make a 15% IRR.

That's not quite as good as I could make as a skilled, experienced active investor in yesterday's market in Denver, but it is close. And it was just my first try, even starting during challenging COVID conditions.

In today's market, with higher interest rates, and very high real estate prices, we can make more as a passive investor nationwide than we can as an active investor in Denver.

What sort of passive investments are we talking about? Let me share two successes and one mistake.

Two great projects and one flop

Our best project was a build-to-rent (BTR) in a suburb of Dallas, Texas. As home prices and interest rates have gone up, many young families that should be first time buyers (FTB) were renting longer than they did in the past. We suspected many of these would-be FTB will end up becoming renters for life.

Since they are getting old enough to have kids and dogs, they no longer wanted to live in a rental house that feels like an apartment complex. They want a garage attached directly to their living space, with a backyard, ideally without someone making noise above them.

The BTR community was a subdivision of duplexes. Instead of being sold to hundreds of individuals, the GP sold the entire community to one Wall Street fund. It was sold before it was finished, as BTR are highly in demand from institutional investors. The LPs got a 56% IRR on this grand slam project.

The next best project was the development of a new luxury apartment complex between Dallas and Fort Worth TX. In the summer of 2022 – with the economy slowing down, a war in Ukraine, massive inflation, and a looming recession – the GP received an unsolicited offer before finishing construction – for more than our pro-forma selling price. The GP accepted, and when construction was complete, we turned over the keys and achieved a 31% annualized IRR for the LPs.

Now, in full disclosure, we must share the worst passive investment, too. The GP bought a distressed office building in a nice suburb of Houston, right before COVID. The plan was to renovate the common areas and vacant office suites. In theory, with better management, we could raise rents, fill the building, then sell it at a good profit.

Great business plan. However, during COVID, not as many companies were interested in leasing space. Supply chain and contractor issues made renovation more costly and take much longer. Nothing went right on this project, and we're hoping to just get our money back (0% IRR), a few years after the initially targeted timeline. More realistically, we may lose some of the initial investment. Our current expected return of 15% annual after expenses assumes we lose all the money on the Houston office project. The power of diversification is that you can have a problem project and still do well overall.

But that's the point; there will always be one investment that doesn't pan out, so you need others to absorb the break even or loss. It's no different than investing in the stock market – not all stocks go up every year, so you diversify.

Understanding Market Strategy

As I write this in June 2024, the commercial market has changed a lot. Most buyers are in "flight to quality" mode. High-quality, high-performance assets such as the two examples above are easy to sell and banks love these loans. But if you have an apartment that is dated, has deferred maintenance, below-market rents and/or high vacancy – it'll be hard to sell, and it'll sell for less than it did two years ago.

Compared to actively managed stock funds which monitor economic trends, interest rates, and many other factors to constantly adjust their portfolio.

Real estate investments move a bit more slowly. The best strategy changes about every 18-24 months, so you must stay on top of the national economics and market trends.

How do the wealthiest families address this?

They have a "family office" (FO) to handle their financial affairs. A FO is a personal financial team that helps wealthy families manage their money and assets. The FO handles everything from investments and taxes to estate planning and philanthropy. They adjust the investment strategy as often as needed to balance risk and returns. The goal is to grow and protect the family's wealth for current and future generations. Family Offices provide tailored financial advice and services, ensuring that the family's financial goals are achieved. A Family Office starts to make sense when you have $50 million or more to manage.

While you definitely need something like that, your assets may not have grown to the size for FO management yet. Most of our readers are in the $1 to $20 million range and instead try to do it on their own. You could go out and find a few passive real estate investments and do the homework for you to determine the optimal strategy, which is always changing. You would also have to write a large check for each individual investment, which puts choice investment-grade properties out of reach for most investors.

But there is a new, little-known option for successful families that do not yet have the assets for a Family Office.

You can have a fund manager that selects and manages a portfolio of real estate investments for you, who finds the deals, makes the site visits, performs the due diligence and communicates with the sponsors for you. (We'll go in-depth into this option more in a moment.)

For example, take those three projects I described earlier. There were eight projects all together in that particular passive portfolio.

Altogether, the eight projects will have around a 15% IRR. The grand-slam BTR project had more than enough profit to make up for the office building mess and that's perfectly normal. That's why we made more investments, to spread out the risk.

Diversification is the key. As a newer active investor, you might have only one or two investments, because that's all you can afford to invest in at one time. That creates <u>a concentration risk</u> of which <u>most investors are completely unaware</u>.

If you are lucky enough to get two great projects, you are off to an amazing start. If you get one good and one bad, your spouse will be unhappy with you. I really like having more investments to diversify and spread the risk. As you will see, the 4 Pillars of Passive Investing will come down to four strategic areas where we diversify to manage risk and then flex with market conditions, and that's always the key to investing.

Types of Diversification

What are these four strategic areas of diversification? Before I went to passive investing, I mostly had residential rentals and some office buildings. My portfolio was concentrated in Denver and in Colorado Springs, and almost all my projects were in the Value-Add strategy (I'll explain this and each strategy below in depth in Chapter 2). What I discovered from my mistakes are the four strategic areas of diversification that *must* be in every fund:

- **Geography**. Currently, 85%+ of the projects we invest in are outside of Colorado, in 15+ different states. While I live in and love Colorado, there are other great spots in the US for real estate investments and we have specific parameters to determine prime investment territory.

- **Asset Class.** Currently, about 35-40% of our projects are outside of the residential asset class. We're invested in warehouses, self-storage, student housing, hospitality, etc.

These are asset types I would not feel comfortable being responsible to manage myself as an active investor.

- **Strategy**. Currently, about half of our projects are new construction. Since I didn't enjoy being a builder, this brings a strategy diversification I was not comfortable doing on my own, but I can access and enjoy as a passive investor.

- **Sponsor**. Now I'm no longer the sole Sponsor/project manager of each project, with all the nitty gritty details, contractors, teams, accounting, etc. which that entails.

In Chapter 2, we will unpack each of these in depth with our specific parameters for each of the 4 Pillars, and how we've made the extensive due diligence process passive for our LPs too. But first, a common question…

Why haven't I heard about this before?

At least weekly, I'll talk to an investor that will say something like "I have an MBA with a Finance concentration, why didn't I learn this then?"

First, what I learned in over 20 years of being an active investor and real estate developer taught me what to look for – and what questions to ask – of the passive investment Sponsors.

Our team feels like we're finally putting our experience to work for us, putting our money to work smarter instead of harder, but we didn't get there overnight. We had to put in our time as active investors first to understand the critical strategies and the exhaustive due diligence that helps us craft well-diversified opportunities.

Second, **there has been a change in legislation which puts these investment grade deals more in the reach of accredited investors.**

The Securities and Exchange Commission (SEC) introduced Rule 506(c) on July 10, 2013, as part of the Jumpstart Our Business Startups (JOBS) Act. The rule allows companies to promote their investments under certain conditions, such as advertising, and allows accredited investors only to participate.

The previous version of Rule 506 allowed private companies to sell equity directly to the public, but it didn't allow for broad promotion. The JOBS Act mandated certain changes to Rule 506 of SEC Regulation D to spur capital formation for growing innovators.

Rule 506(c) allows issuers to issue an unlimited number of securities, and to broadly solicit and advertise an offering, <u>provided that all purchasers in the offering are accredited investors</u>. The issuer must also take reasonable steps to verify purchasers' accredited investor status, and certain other conditions in Regulation D are satisfied.

The new law also enabled the ability for General Partners (GPs) of real estate investments to raise money from Limited Partners (LPs), but it took several years for the new idea to catch on. (We'll go more into the roles of GPs and LPs in depth in Chapter 4.)

Is it really easier to invest in passive projects?

The ongoing daily work is immeasurably easier! However, the up-front due diligence work is about the same, or slightly more difficult. First, it is important to only partner with local Sponsors with deep expertise. They must be thoroughly vetted out to ensure they have the experience to run the projects profitably to completion.

For example, one Sponsor we've invested with ONLY does multifamily, heavy value-add of 1970's and 1980's properties, and only in Texas, Alabama, Georgia, and Florida. The first project we invested with them was their 55th project, and their 25th specifically in FL. We still went to physically visit the property to understand it completely. We went through the spreadsheeting in detail and checked the financial models. And we spend a lot of time getting to know the Sponsors while we're on site, in person. We're trading more work up-front for less work managing the project.

Of course, in retrospect, knowing what I know now, I could have done it better and faster. That's why I'm sharing what we've learned with you!

Overall, I've met some amazing people, really improved a lot of properties, and made some great returns along the way. My wife retired early last year, but I love what I do too much to retire. It's nice to have the time and ability to choose, and not have my finances force the decision on me.

Now, let me unpack what I've learned about the 4 Pillars of Passive Real Estate Investing, so you and your family can enjoy the lifestyle and time you so richly deserve for your hard work over the years.

Chapter 2: The Four Pillars of Passive Investing

Now, you'll likely have heard of these four pillars separately, so you know they are true, and the secret is in the implementation and market timing.

After all, a key difference between an amateur and an expert investor comes down to the experience know how to diversify, and to track the trends and translate that into an actionable (and accountable) investment strategy, which will then need to be updated as the market trends change.

Pillar 1: Diversify Geography

Among the four types of diversification, I find that this one is the easiest for newer investors to understand. Before passive investing, I was 100% geographically allocated to Colorado. I was even further concentrated just in Denver and in Colorado Springs.

Then, in 2023 alone, the Colorado Legislature passed nine new laws that all favored the tenant and were not in the interest of the landlord, which has made investing in Colorado extremely difficult.

For example, tenants now have a right of first refusal to renew their lease. If you are an active investor – have you ever had a problem tenant? Perhaps they usually paid late, created a lot of wear and tear on the unit, were loud, messy and/or annoyed the other nice tenants in the building? And I know you've had some tenants that checked ALL these boxes. Me too! I couldn't wait for their lease to expire so I could find a better tenant. Now I can't make that decision! The tenant decides if they want to renew, not me.

There are several more bills that passed in 2024 like this one. Colorado has gone from an investor-neutral to an investor-hostile state in three short years. If I still had all my investment in Colorado alone, I'd be facing a significant increase in business risk, not to mention more grey hair and lower returns on my investment.

This change in the regulatory environment can happen at any time, anywhere. If you can spread out the geographic footprint of your portfolio, you can greatly reduce your exposure to these shifts.

Currently, we focus on the sunbelt states. Why? They have the most population growth and reasonable real estate policies.

Population growth is the biggest driver of a local real estate market. Population is declining in Chicago, New York state, and parts of California. There isn't demand for new homes or apartments. There's a little less interest each year to buy a house, so there is no upward pressure on prices to drive appreciation.

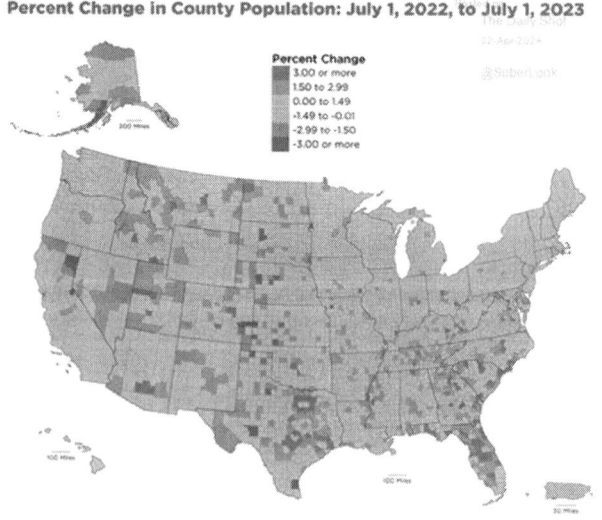

Map source: Census Bureau.

On the other hand, markets with population growth need new development. The increase in population means more competition among consumers to buy a home or rent an apartment, which drives appreciation and cashflow growth.

Let's look at the average home price appreciation from 1991-2023.

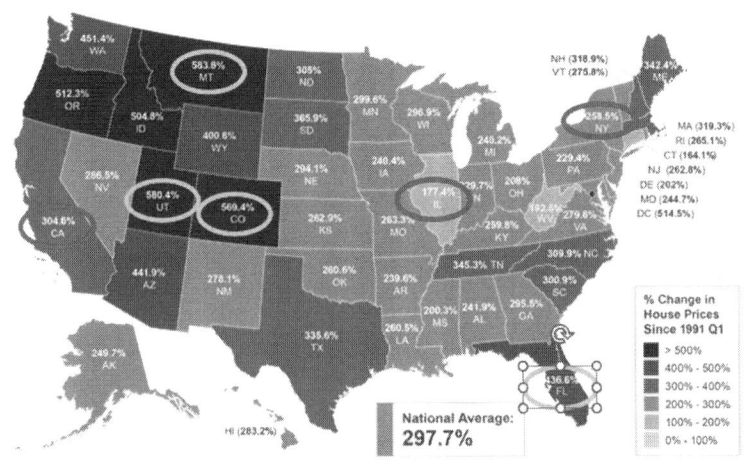

Map Source: FHFA | Federal Housing Finance Agency

States with strong population growth like Utah, Colorado, Arizona, Montana, and Florida all had appreciation that exceeded the US average of 297% from 1991 to 2023.

States with stagnant or declining population, like New York and Illinois, had below average appreciation. California is in the middle; it's growing at a much slower pace. And California's appreciation, as you might expect, is right about at the US average.

The pace of population relocations seems to be accelerating post-COVID. This could be a function of greater acceptance of remote work.

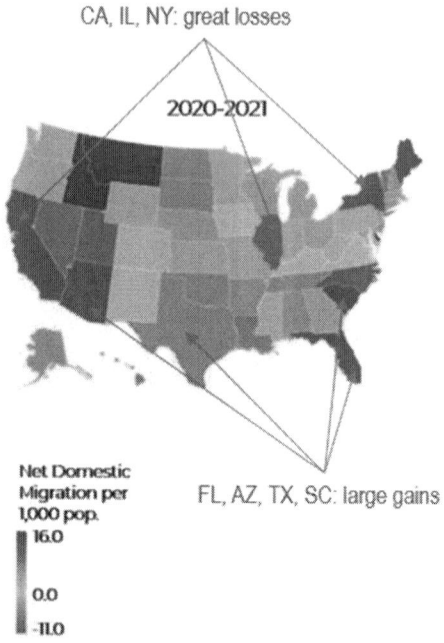

CA, IL, NY: great losses

2020-2021

Net Domestic Migration per 1,000 pop.

16.0

0.0

-11.0

FL, AZ, TX, SC: large gains

Source: US Census.

Another way to identify population movement is to monitor which states have the most in-bound U-Haul traffic.

State	2023 Rank	2022 Rank
Texas	1	1
Florida	2	2
North Carolina	3	4
South Carolina	4	3
Tennessee	5	6
Idaho	6	10
Washington	7	23
Arizona	8	7
Colorado	9	11
Virginia	10	5

Source: U-Haul.

All of these states are among what we consider our 15 top markets.

Pillar 2: Diversify Asset Class

Investors also need to diversify by asset class. While each expert will slice the real estate universe into slightly different wedges, here's the way we like to separate deals:

1. Residential
-   Single family homes and condos.

2. Multifamily
-   The term "multifamily real estate" comprises all residential real estate, except for single-family homes.
-   Multifamily properties are subdivided into Class A, Class B, and Class C properties depending on their location, condition, and more. "A" is nicer or the nicest.
-   Most leases are for a year and the tenant doesn't demand customization of their space.

3. Office
-   They range from single-story suburban buildings to multi-story urban buildings.
-   Most office buildings are developed for multiple tenants, investors generate several revenue streams.
-   This provides income diversity, helping investors to retain cashflow even if a tenant terminates a lease.
-   Compared to other types of commercial real estate properties, office leases tend to be longer, too. 3-5 years for a "C" building and 5-10 years for an "A" building.
-   In most markets, leases customarily come with built-in annual inflation increases each year.
-   In some markets, the leases are triple net (see next section for an overview of triple net leases).
-   New tenants often demand their space to be customized, which is cost to the landlord (and significant project management time, too).

4. Industrial
- Attractive investment due to their long-term return and leases, as well as low overhead costs.
- Often "triple-net" (or NNN), where the tenant, not the landlord, is responsible for maintenance, utilities, taxes. This makes management easy. It's the closest thing to "mailbox money."
- Several types of industrial buildings, which vary in size, layout, format, and typical tenant, provide further opportunities for the investor to diversify.
- However, the rent increases customarily are usually not as large as other office and multifamily buildings.

5. Retail
- Occupied by businesses offering products and services to customers, including stores, and restaurants.
- Amazon and other online stores caused retail foot traffic to decline, but this type of commercial real estate still plays an important role.
- Like office and industrial, leases are much longer than residential. Inflation increases are usually built in.
- Like office, retail tenants often expect the landlord to customize their space.

6. Hotels & Hospitality
- Offer both short- and long-term accommodations to travelers, both for leisure or business purposes.
- There are many segments, from economy to luxury, and from very short (nightly) stays to extended stays.
- Higher returns, but higher headaches. You really are managing a business AND a property.

7. Land
- One of the riskiest types of commercial real estate.
- Historically, offers the highest return.

8. Mixed Use
-   Properties that combine two or more of the above.
-   Many downtown high-rises are considered mixed use.
-   These often have retail on the first few floors and offices, hotels, or apartments above.

9. Self-Storage
-   Low cost to operate.
-   Very short lease durations.

Initially, all my investments were residential. That's how most new investors get started in real estate. Midway through my investing career, I started to sell several smaller condos and townhomes to buy commercial properties like warehouses and office buildings.

This greatly reduced the number of buildings I had to track. Even with property managers for all of them, there is work involved in managing the manager.

Office buildings in Denver were a good investment before COVID in 2020. Post-COVID, most office buildings are experiencing increased vacancy rates, and higher concessions to attract tenants. Medical offices are a notable exception. If you have all your money tied up in one asset class, an event like COVID can really change your outlook.

I now have about 65% of my personal real estate investments in residential and multifamily. Historically, these asset classes have the lowest returns among the different commercial choices. The offset is they have the least volatility. That means even in a downturn, they perform well.

Example 1: Some sub-sectors do even better in a recession than in a growing economy. These are called counter-cyclical. For example, many apartment renters will need to trade down in the amount of space they can afford, or move in with a roommate, during a recession. As a result, self-storage often has an uptick in demand in a recession.

Example 2: More luxurious hospitality offerings perform well in an economic expansion, but are among the first of the corporate and personal spending items that get cut back in a recession. The economy segment of hospitality often takes share from the more expensive hotels in a recession.

This is why it's not enough to simply choose a couple set asset classes for diversification and stay there. To truly manage your risk, you must keep your finger on the pulse of the market and be ready to shift into emerging assets as their time comes. This is why we have monthly live updates on the state of the market so you can be in position as the market trends change.

*****

As our gift to you to help you on your investing journey, go to https://irontoncapital.com/marketupdates to get invited to our next live update.

Pillar 3: Diversify Strategy

Investors also need to diversify across Strategy. There are three broad strategic categories you can select when building your real estate portfolio.

- Buy and Hold (aka "Rental" or "Income")
- Improvement (aka "Value Add")
- Development (aka "New Build")

An important concept for how to choose between them is determined by your risk tolerance.

Risk tolerance in investing refers to an investor's ability to handle fluctuations in the value of their investments. It's like knowing how much uncertainty or ups and downs in the stock market you can handle without feeling uncomfortable or making rash decisions.

Factors like age, financial goals, and personal feelings about risk all play a role in determining your risk tolerance.

For example, younger investors may be more willing to take on higher risks in exchange for potentially higher returns, while older investors nearing retirement may prefer more conservative investments to protect their savings.

Buy and Hold

When people first think of real estate investing, this is the first strategy that they hear about. Buy and Hold properties are properties in great condition, being managed well, and providing a reliable cashflow. They may or may not be in a great location.

These are often newer properties, or older properties that have just come off a significant renovation program and are in great shape. You can purchase a property like this easily on your own.

A more practical – and tax advantageous – method is to purchase some shares in a REIT (Real Estate Investment Trust). This enables you to get a diversified portfolio of many properties (usually all in the buy and hold strategy, and in one asset class, but in many locations). REITs have a tax advantage for many people, in that their income is usually taxed at a lower rate than your marginal income tax rate (especially if you are in a higher tax bracket – ask your CPA for additional information).

Another great thing about REITs is that many of them are publically traded (like the stock market), so you can buy and sell (e.g., have access to liquidity) on a much more flexible basis than if you own the underlying assets directly.

A downside to REITs is that they are not allowed to pass along depreciation (a passive tax write off for many investors) to their owners. Directly owning real estate allows you to get access to that depreciation.

Finally, non-recourse loans can often be available for REITs and large (over $5 MM) multifamily loans. That is, you may not have to personally guarantee the loan if something goes wrong or the market changes. There are a whole host of pros and cons, but many larger investors do like non-recourse loans. Lenders for smaller investments almost always require personal guarantees.

Advantages of Buy and Hold
- Cashflows right away.
- Generally, the lowest risk of the real estate strategies.
- Most predictable cashflow.
- Easiest to finance, and usually on great terms.
- Often, non-recourse lending is an option if loan size is large; else personal guarantee likely will be needed.
- Easiest to sell.
- Smallest need for special expertise to do well.
- May offer depreciation tax write-offs if you invest directly.
- Often, pride of ownership.
- If in a REIT, you can buy and sell easily, almost like trading stocks.

Disadvantages of Buy and Hold
- Most expensive to purchase.
- Lowest return on investment.
- May not offer depreciation tax write-off if via a REIT.
- Often, least upside for above-average appreciation.

In summary: Safer, less work, and less return.

Value-Add

Next, Value-Add properties are those which are not in great condition. Any property, without constant care and thoughtful oversight, will eventually devolve from a pristine Buy and Hold to a Value-Add project. This might be in condition of the units themselves, the common areas, or both. They may also have poor management and/or deferred maintenance in the infrastructure (e.g., elevators, HVAC systems).

A common way this happens is when an active investor buys a property and has the energy to keep it in top quality condition. As they age, health problems interfere with their ability to take care of the investment. Their spouse and/or kids usually lack the passion and expertise to provide the right oversight to the property manager. Since by this point their mortgage is either paid off, or has a minimal payment, there is no urgency to maximize the cashflow.

There is a strong incentive to pass property to your heirs. If the older owner dies, their kids will inherit the property (assuming the estate plan is set up this way). If they purchased it for $1 million thirty years ago, it might be worth $5 million today. If they sold it while they were alive, they would owe tax on a $4 million capital gain (plus depreciation recapture, which we will discuss in a later chapter).

If their kids inherit it, usually they will be able to get an appraisal for the value at the time of their death. That becomes their tax basis in the property. So, their starting point is now $5 million. They can sell the next day for $5 million, and no capital gains (or depreciation recapture) are due. This is the among the best ways to transfer wealth between generations.

All the while, the property has degraded, has more deferred maintenance, and usually low occupancy and below-market rents. The kids often just dump the property ASAP after the probate process is wrapped up. These properties will often trade at a significant discount to what the same size buy and hold property will sell for. Not all Value-Add properties follow this path, but many do.

One additional attractive dimension of Value-Add projects is the depreciation. You can think of depreciation as an interest-free loan from the IRS. For a residential property, you can "depreciate" it over 27.5 years.

Initial Value	$4,000,000
Land	$1,250,000
Improvements	$2,750,000
Years	27.50
Depreciation / Year	$100,000

Your CPA can help you split up the value of your purchase between the land and the improvements (e.g., the building). In this example, you would write off $100,000 per year.

From the IRS point of view, it is as if you wrote a check to some vendor for that amount, and it reduces your income (and tax bill) that year. Since you don't write this check, you get to keep the cash without the tax. When you sell the property, you must true up with the IRS (which is called "depreciation recapture). For an older property, you can often accelerate the depreciation to generate even larger write-offs in the first year or two. I'll cover this in more detail later in the book.

Advantages of Value-Add Projects
- Much less expensive to purchase.
- Much higher potential return on investment if you know what you are doing or hire an experienced team.
- Depreciation tax write-offs.
- Potentially large passive loss write-offs.

Disadvantages of Value-Add Projects
- Limited, or negative, cashflow to start.
- A significant renovation budget is usually needed.
- Usually requires a construction loan vs. more favorable long-term financing.
- Recourse financing is almost always required.
- Project management and turn-around property management specialists required.

In summary: More work, more risk, and much higher returns.

Development

Finally, Development projects are building a property from scratch. You'd first need to do a demand study to be sure that your project would be right for the location.

For example, if you wanted to build a new economy extended-stay hotel, you'd do a study to determine:

- The current demand for lodging in that market
- How that was disaggregated across different hospitality sectors
- What the likely growth of the market is projected to be

In this example, you'd love to see that 18% of the stays in the market are over seven nights (e.g., extended stay), but that only

10% of the available hotel beds in the market are configured as extended stay hotels (e.g., the rooms have mini-kitchens and other amenities for longer term guests). There's a lot more to a demand analysis, of course, but this illustrates it at a high level.

Once you know there is demand for what you want to build, you'd look for land that would be appropriate to serve that need. The starting point could be:

Raw land
- Cheapest to purchase.
- May or may not have the correct zoning in place.
- May involve a lengthy process with local government planning authority to get permits (to build).
- Often the longest project, with highest risk, and on average, highest returns.
- Usually, you will not be able to generate income while you are holding it, so you need to have more reserves to make bank interest payments and pay property taxes while you go through the zoning and permitting process.

Improved land
- Intermediate cost of the three development options.
- Already zoned correctly.
- May have some/all the pre-construction design and engineering complete.
- In some cases, projects are sold "shovel ready" where you can pull the permit and start right away.
- No surprise: Lower risk, faster timelines, and lower returns than raw land.
- Fewer holding costs before construction.

Existing site
- Demolish ("scrape") an existing building and replace it with something new (usually a lot bigger).

- Often zoned correctly but might require some of the re-zoning steps in "raw land."
- Many times, the existing building can generate cashflow to offset holding costs while you navigate the paperwork with the government.

If you are highly confident that you'll (eventually) get your government approvals, you can work on the other development tasks in parallel to save time.

Some sample tasks would include:
- Environmental reviews
- Soil testing and civil engineering (to design the foundation)
- Architectural and engineering design for the building
- Sharing these reports with general contractors to get bids
- Meeting with banks to explain the project, assess interest, and gather term sheets

Once you have your permits (you are "shovel ready"), you can close on the loan with the bank and get started. Either you will need to be on site frequently to assess progress, quality check, and solve the innumerable problems that come up, or have an "owners rep" that does all of this for you.

I'm continually amazed at how many people have an interest in becoming a real estate developer. It sounds sexy to people, for some reason, but it really is a lot of work. There is a big satisfaction at the end when you see the finished product (especially if you managed to make a profit in the process), and that's likely the appeal.

Advantages of Development
- Very high potential return on investment if you know what you are doing and/or hire an experienced team.
- Most problem solving and potential for creative solutions if that's what you enjoy.

Disadvantages of Development
- Limited, or negative, cashflow to start.
- Always requires a construction loan vs. more favorable long-term financing.
- Recourse financing is almost always required.
- Advanced project management and turn-around property management specialists required.
- No depreciation in early years for passive losses.
- Not recommended if you can't handle stress.
- Has the most problem solving if you are NOT into that.

In summary: The highest effort, highest risk, and highest returns.

There are as many ways to build a real estate portfolio as there are ways to build a stock portfolio. I personally am not interested in Buy and Hold since I have the experience to pursue the two more advanced strategies that generate much high returns in most economic environments. Everyone will have a different perspective on this.

Pillar 4: Diversify Sponsors

Finally, investors need to diversify their Sponsors. An often-overlooked fact is that the active investor IS the Sponsor. If you make a mistake on one of your properties, it might be the same type of oversight you made on many of the properties in your portfolio. Every Sponsor has their strengths and weaknesses.

If you have multiple investments with multiple Sponsors, you are diversifying this hidden risk.

Let me share an example from my experience that still makes me cringe. We made an investment with a General Partner (GP) that partnered with a property management (PM) company. It turns out that the PM was experienced, but they had never worked with the specific type of project that this GP specialized in. The GP assumed – and we did too – that this PM would be able to easily morph to handle this slightly different type of asset.

Turns out we were all wrong. The PM didn't do a great job. There were several confounding factors. The PM initially explained it away as a change in market conditions. Honestly, we thought it was plausible too. The GP ended up giving more time to a PM that really was not right for this project. The GP eventually had to replace them. Since the GP had a deep relationship with that PM across a LOT of projects, this was a messy business divorce. It distracted the GP and the PM from their core jobs of managing renovations, contractors, and getting new tenants at higher rents into newly refinished rental units.

The turnaround wound up taking a lot longer than it should. The longer the project takes, the lower the rate of return or IRR.

Imagine you made ten investments in your portfolio, and all ten were with this GP (this GP has over 30 projects, all in the Value-Add strategy). Your entire portfolio would be at risk.

Ideally, you would have many investments with many different GPs. Each GP will have their own idiosyncratic deficiencies and blind spots, but they are unlikely to overlap!

In summary, you want to be mindful of creating a balanced portfolio across all 4 Pillars of Diversification. This is what can enable you to generate strong returns in the 17-20% annual range while having a well-managed level of risk.

Many of our readers are professionals that have invested in many years of education and working to develop their expertise. Real estate investing is its own specialty and requires the same care and time to build expertise for profitable returns. For many, building that expertise creates another part- to full-time job that they just do not have time to add into their already busy lives.

That's why many have discovered passive investing to, essentially, hire the expert to do what they do best and instead focus on their lives and families and retire on their own timetable.

Now let's dive into some real-life case studies and we'll see the 4 Pillars of Diversification in Action!

*****

Our Investor Relations team has set aside some time for you if you would like to see if passive investing is right for you. Go to http://irontoncapital.com/gopassive to choose your best time for your free portfolio review.

Chapter 3: The Four Pillars in Action!

What does it look like when we take the 4 Pillars to create one of our diversified funds? Let's look at Ironton Capital's National Diversified Fund 5 (NDF5) for an example of how this diversification works.

Here is how the distribution of four pillars looks like in our NDF5:

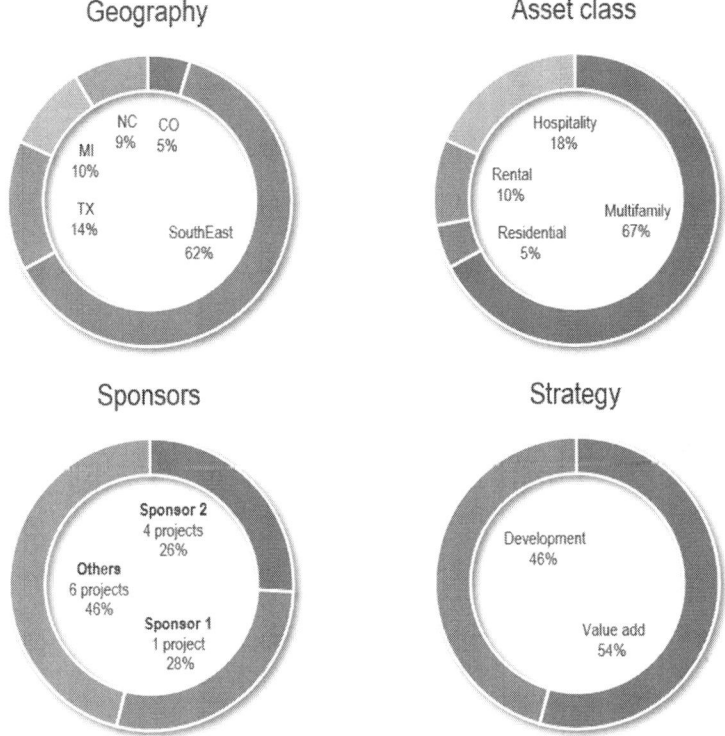

This is a long-term investment with an expected horizon of 5-6 years. You'll see that we're spread across a good deal of the US. We're in 4 different asset classes that are advantageous in the current and projected market conditions. We're working with more than eight Sponsors deployed in 2 different Strategies.

Now, let's look at the projected returns:

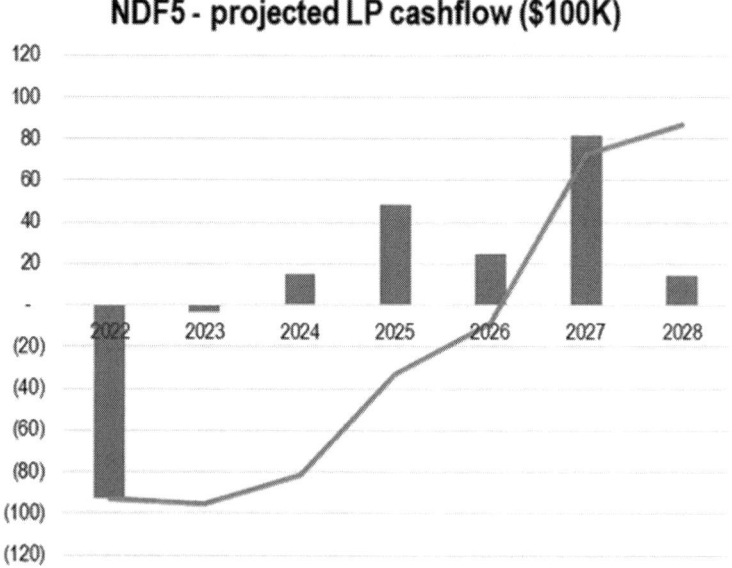

NDF5 - projected LP cashflow ($100K)

This chart shows the investments are made mostly in 2022, and most of the returns are expected in 2025 and 2027.

NDF5 expects to generate annualized returns of 17-20% per year (IRR, internal rate of return), after all fees and expenses, for our investors. The fund was launched in the fall of 2022. As of this writing (June 2024), one of the eleven investments has already been realized. Its return of 22.7% was slightly ahead of pro-forma.

We made eleven investments. Some of the investments have multiple assets. For example, the first one is a developer of new workforce housing apartments. Most new construction for apartments is in the luxury class. Typical residents have rather high-end, high-income jobs. Not everyone can afford this. Workforce housing is designed for people at the area median income. Typical residents are firefighters, teachers, and police officers.

Photo Copyright: Ironton Capital

Despite being aimed at lower, median-income residents; the units are still quite nice.

Photo Copyright: Ironton Capital

The developer will build about 25 apartment communities (of 200-300 units in each community) across three different states.

- Geography: Florida, South Carolina, Georgia
- Asset class: Multifamily
- Strategy: New construction

Three of the investments are with a multifamily Value-Add specialist. Each investment is in one large apartment complex. In each case, the prior owner neglected the property, leading to deferred maintenance, poor unit quality, and suboptimal management. The Sponsor renovates the unit interiors, fixes deferred maintenance, and makes investments in common area upgrades.

RENOVATED  UNRENOVATED

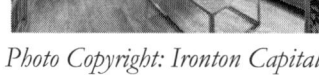

Photo Copyright: Ironton Capital

A new management team combined with new digital and social media strategies greatly increases the flow of prospective new residents. Rents, which are $400-500 per month below market, have increased, greatly improving the cashflow performance.

- **Geography**: Plano & Fort Worth, TX; St Petersburg, FL
- **Asset class**: Multifamily
- **Strategy**: Value-Add

As a final example, another Sponsor is building six new hotels. They are focused on the budget, extended-stay segment. Nationally, about 18% of the nights in hotels are for stays over a week-long (which is the definition of extended stay). Yet only around 10% of the hotels in the US are configured for the needs of these types of travelers (e.g., have a small kitchen in the room). The Sponsor did a study to find where the needs of extended travelers are most underserved and picked six of the best markets.

The focus is on the budget segment for several reasons:
- These hotels are easy to operate with just a few employees.
- They are quick to achieve break-even economics.
- The break-even occupancy point is relatively low.
- They are quick and easy to build.
- There is a lot of demand among institutional buyers to purchase these types of hotels once they are completed and have a year or so of operating history.
- This budget segment is the most recession-proof within the hospitality industry. In a recession, luxury travelers will trade down as their budgets are constrained.

There's another compelling reason for the budget extended stay segment. Many of these guests travel regardless of the economic situation. According to our partner Sponsor, here's the national guest mix for 7+ night stays:

- 28% are travelling workers. Travelling nurses are the most famous example. They fill short term staffing shortages at hospitals and clinics.
  Another example is utility workers. When a large snowstorm knocks down power lines, utility works from several states will send in a swarm of workers to help get the lights back on. Often several weeks are needed to make the repairs. Recession or not, these workers are on the road.
- 17% are relocated workers. While they wait to close on their new home or move into their new apartment, they will spend some time at an extended stay hotel.
- 17% are home transition. A family might sell their old home and plan to immediately move into a new construction home. If there is a delay in construction, the family ends up in an extended stay hotel for a time.

There are other segments, but this illustrates it well.
- **Geography:** Texas, Alabama, Florida
- **Asset class:** Hospitality
- **Strategy:** New construction

Overall, NDF5 has just over forty commercial properties in ten different states. It's well diversified to manage risks while still generating strong returns.

Up to this point, we've given you the foundation for passive, real estate investing and real-world examples of how we implement them. Now, let's build a plan using the 4 Pillars of Diversification so you can put them to work for you!

*****

If you would like to speak with our Investor Relations team to see if passive investing is right for you, then go to http://irontoncapital.com/gopassive to choose your best time.

Chapter 4: Putting the 4 Pillars to Work for You!

If you've peeked at the appendix on active investing, you'll have seen that passive investing is a whole lot easier. You've also seen that through the 4 Pillars of Diversification, the risk is highly managed. But how does a busy individual, like yourself, find 8+ different investments for your passive portfolio?

That's exactly why we founded Ironton Capital, and it all starts with syndication.

What is Syndication?

A real estate syndication is when a group of people pool their money together to invest in a real estate project. It's like teamwork – each person contributes money, and together they buy properties such as apartment buildings, shopping centers, or an office building.

One benefit is that it allows investors to invest in larger properties or projects that they might not be able to afford on their own. It also spreads out the risks because if one property doesn't do well, the losses, as well as the wins, are shared among all the investors. Additionally, real estate syndications often provide passive income through rental payments or property appreciation.

There can also be some drawbacks.
-   There are often just one or two properties, which doesn't bring much diversification to balance risk.
-   Investors usually have limited control over the property and its management decisions since those are typically handled by a designated manager or Sponsor. This is usually a drawback for

Private Equity (PE) Funds, too, as you'll see in the next
section.
-   Investments will usually be highly illiquid, meaning it can be
    challenging to sell your share of the property if you need to
    access your money quickly. This applies to PE, too.
-   Like any investment, there are risks involved, such as
    fluctuations in the real estate market or unexpected expenses.

Before the SEC enabled private equity funds to be more broadly
available about a decade ago, syndications were the primary
method by which investors got access to passive real estate
projects.

What is a Private Equity fund?

What is a private equity (PE) fund? It is a type of investment that
collects money from investors to buy and manage properties.

It's like a big pool of money that's used to purchase real estate
assets such as apartment buildings, office spaces, or shopping
centers. The PE fund can purchase the properties directly, or the
PE fund can invest in Sponsors, who are directly hands-on with the
real estate.

The fund is managed by a team of professionals who make
decisions about which properties to buy, how to improve them,
and when to sell them for a profit.

Advantages:
-   It allows passive investors to invest in real estate without
    having to buy and manage properties themselves.
-   It provides diversification because the PE fund may invest in a
    variety of properties across different locations and sectors,
    spreading out the risk.

- Ironton's National Diversified Funds (NDF), for example, will have 30-40 properties in a fund.
- Investors can benefit from professional management expertise and potentially higher returns than they might achieve on their own.

Disadvantages:
- Investors typically have limited control over the fund's investment decisions, as they are made by the fund manager.
- Real estate private equity funds often require a significant initial investment and have longer investment horizons, meaning your money may be tied up for several years.
- Like any investment, there are risks involved, such as market fluctuations, economic downturns, and the potential for losses.

And remember, it is essential for investors to carefully consider their risk tolerance and investment goals before participating in a real estate private equity fund or any investment. Always talk to your financial advisors.

How Does a Private Equity Fund Work?

There are several parties involved in this form of investment to make it go smoothly. Let's explore everyone's role.

Limited Partner (LP)
Individual Passive Investor like You

Here are the most common tasks for the LP:
- Chooses Fund (GP)
- Decides investment size
- Reads quarterly reports
- Re-invests or Deposits returns
- Enjoys passive financial freedom

General Partner (GP)
Private Equity Fund Manager like Ironton Capital

Here are the most common tasks for the GP:

- Monitors national & local markets
  - o Networks to identify opportunities; often the best deals are off-market and are found via networking
  - o Reviews multiple projects
  - o Selects optimal investments
  - o Negotiates favorable deals
- Performs extensive due diligence
  - o Sponsor reputation and track record
  - o Financial, operational, and additional aspects
  - o Site visits
  - o Detailed Financial modeling
- Maintains regulatory compliance
- Maintains accounting records; coordinates taxes; research tax-optimizing strategies
- Quarterly reporting to LPs

Sponsor Property Management for the Investment

Here are the most common tasks for the Sponsor:

- Selects the physical project
- Arranges and guarantees the financing
- Re-zones property if needed
- Arranges construction and engineering permits
- Oversees construction or renovation
- Manages the property
  - o Finds and manages the tenants
  - o Maintains the property
  - o Manages the legalities
- Manages refinancing
- Manages the sales process
- Maintains consistent quarterly reporting to the GP

When you invest in Private Equity (PE) fund, it is like investing in a mutual fund with an active manager that researches the economy and picks individual stocks to match the investor's investment strategy. The PE fund adds a layer of expense in exchange for professional experience and expertise. The PE fund then picks individual Sponsors that are hands-on with the real estate in investments.

If you like to research and pick out your own stocks, without a mutual fund, that is like skipping the PE fund layer, and investing directly in the real estate Sponsors. That legal form is called a "Syndication" that we described earlier. There's less expense for the passive investor, but a lot more work.

What's best? It depends on what you enjoy, what your skills are, and what is the next best use of your time.

Fees and Expenses

Real estate private equity funds typically charge fees to cover management and operational expenses. These fees can vary depending on the fund's structure and investment strategy but commonly include:

- Acquisition Fees:
  - Some real estate private equity funds charge fees for identifying and acquiring properties.
  - These fees may vary based on the size and complexity of the transaction.

- Management Fees:
  - These fees are charged annually and are typically a percentage of the total assets under management, ranging from 1% to 3%.

o They cover the costs of fund management, including salaries, office expenses, and administrative costs.

- Performance Fees (also known as "carried interest" or "carry"):
  o Performance fees are typically a percentage of the profits earned by the fund, often around 20%.
  o These fees are charged only if the fund achieves certain performance benchmarks, such as surpassing a specified rate of return or reaching a certain profit threshold.
  o Performance fees incentivize the fund manager to achieve strong investment results.
  o Usually, the investor gets paid first with a "preferred return."

- Other Fees:
  o Additional fees may include expenses such as legal fees, due diligence costs, and fund administration fees.

It's important for investors to carefully review the fee structure of a real estate private equity fund before investing, and to understand how these fees may impact their overall returns.

There are four offsets to these PE Fund expenses:
1. When a PE fund makes a large investment in a Sponsor, the fund can usually negotiate better terms than a small passive investor.
   - This is called a "side letter."
   - These savings are usually not enough to offset all the PE fees, but may offset a meaningful portion of the fees.

2. Most Sponsors would prefer to work with a smaller number of large investors (e.g., PE firms), and not hundreds of smaller "retail" passive investors.
   - As a result, the larger investors see many more of the best opportunities than the smaller passive investors.

- For a given amount of investment risk, these "off market" opportunities often have better returns than the typical deals in the passive investment market.
- This is where the PE funds earn their fees.

3. Most Sponsors have a "friends and family" list.
   - When they have a small deal with great economics, it is never broadly circulated.
   - The inner group of friends sees it and fulfills the investment need.
   - Outsiders are only brought in when the inner group doesn't raise sufficient capital.
   - Established PE firms often have access to these deals.

4. Finally, there are short-term opportunities where a Sponsor needs to raise cash rapidly for an unusually good opportunity.
   - The investors that the Sponsor has found to be reliable in the past are quick to decide and deliver funds get called first.
   - The attractive return on these special situations usually ensures only a small number of large investors are needed before the funding is raised.
   - PE firms spend a lot of time networking to establish the relationships to get access to these investments.

Now that you know about the two options for investing passively, let's look at how you can fund the investments.

Should I Use Cash?

For many of our readers, cash is the easiest way to invest passively. The long-term investment funds like Ironton's National Diversified Funds (NDFs) are optimized to deliver mostly capital gains, and minimize the amount distributed as ordinary income. For most investors, this is best for their tax situation.

Using cash may give you the opportunity to use depreciation to offset some of your passive gains. (We'll go over this in more detail later.)

If you need income, our Short Term Income fund (STI) is structured as a REIT (Real Estate Investment Trust). For most investors, REITs are taxed at a lower rate than their marginal income rate. The higher your tax bracket, the more the potential savings.

Check with your CPA to discover if this can help your family.

Should I Unlock My Home Equity?

If your primary residence or vacation home has a lot of equity, you might be able to use a HELOC (home equity line of credit) or some other type of second mortgage to access your equity. If you can borrow at 5-7% and invest at 17%+, you will create a lot of wealth over time.

Here's a greatly simplified example:

Imagine you borrow at 7%, and your bank allows you to let the balance increase over time vs. making payments. That's an oversimplification, but it'll get us started. If you borrowed $100,000, your debt would grow to $197,000 over a decade.

	Borrow HELOC 7.00%	Invest NDF 17.00%	Invest MTI 12.00%
Year 0	$100,000	$100,000	$100,000
Year 1	$107,000	$117,000	$112,000
Year 2	$114,490	$136,890	$125,440
Year 3	$122,504	$160,161	$140,493
Year 4	$131,080	$187,389	$157,352
Year 5	$140,255	$219,245	$176,234
Year 6	$150,073	$256,516	$197,382
Year 7	$160,578	$300,124	$221,068
Year 8	$171,819	$351,145	$247,596
Year 9	$183,846	$410,840	$277,308
Year 10	$196,715	$480,683	$310,585
Net gain		**$283,968**	**$113,870**

If you invested that $100,000 in the NDF (National Diversified Fund), our goal is to deliver 17-20% annual returns. Over a decade, a $100,000 investment at a 17% return could grow to $481,000. That's a $284,000 pre-tax profit, net of your HELOC cost. Of course, past performance is not a predictor of future results.

Note that some, or perhaps all, of your HELOC interest might be deductible, potentially against your ordinary income in a high tax bracket. Those deductions might occur each year, as a near-term benefit (talk to your CPA).

On the other hand, most of the NDF profit would be taxed as a long-term capital gain. For most of our readers, that will be a lower tax rate, and the gain will come near the end of the life of the investment. Talk to your CPA, but the after-tax impact could be better than these pre-tax numbers suggest.

Be aware that the NDFs are not liquid. You can't access your investment like you could with a stock mutual fund. IF you need liquidity, you might invest instead in the STI or our Medium Term

Income Fund (MTI). It has much more liquidity than NDFs. It could return 12% per year and grow to $311,000 in value over a decade. In this example, you would keep $114,000 net of your HELOC cost.

Note these are not guarantees, and actual investment performance may be different. We are not financial advisors, so please consider these with your CPA and other team members.

Let's look at a slightly more detailed example. Let's imagine you borrow on your HELOC and must make a payment each year. You use the quarterly dividends from the MTI fund to make that interest payment, and you re-invest the extra proceeds, so the balance grows over time.

End of Year	Borrow HELOC at 7%	HELOC interest	Invest in MTI at 12%	Gross MTI dividend	Dividend net of HELOC interest
Zero	$100,000		$100,000		
1	$100,000	$7,000	$105,000	$12,000	$5,000
2	$100,000	$7,000	$110,600	$12,600	$5,600
3	$100,000	$7,000	$116,872	$13,272	$6,272
4	$100,000	$7,000	$123,897	$14,025	$7,025
5	$100,000	$7,000	$131,764	$14,868	$7,868
6	$100,000	$7,000	$140,576	$15,812	$8,812
7	$100,000	$7,000	$150,445	$16,869	$9,869
8	$100,000	$7,000	$161,498	$18,053	$11,053
9	$100,000	$7,000	$173,878	$19,380	$12,380
10	$100,000	$7,000	$187,744	$20,865	$13,865
	Gain, net of HELOC		**$87,744**		

This approach generates a total return of nearly $188,000 on your $100,000 that you borrowed. After you pay back the $100,000 loan, you have nearly $88,000 left over.

If mortgage interest rates are relatively high, that may reduce returns. Even so, this approach can make a lot of sense for many investors. When rates are in decline, this strategy is even more attractive!

*****

If you would like to talk to one of our Investor Relations team about how these scenarios might work for you, so you can investigate it further with your CPA, then go to http://irontoncapital.com/gopassive to choose your best time for your free portfolio review.

How to get off the 1031 treadmill!

If you own active rentals now, even if you use a property manager to help, it's a lot of work. You might have a lot of equity tied up in the properties. You may be ready to offload the properties and the work, but how do retain your tax advantages without 1031 exchanges or a Delaware Statutory Trust (DST)?

There are several well-known options to unlock your equity.

You may be able to talk to your bank to get a second mortgage to access the equity, just as we illustrated for your primary residence or second home.

Another option is to sell the investment property, pay the capital gains, and redeploy the funds in different investments. If you are tired of being an active investor – even with the assistance of a property manager – this can be a great option for you.

Many investors initially hesitate about the capital gains tax. Let's look at the actual numbers in a real-life case study from a recent investor that we helped. This investor purchased a rental property for $187,000 and did a $9,300 renovation. She purchased the property in 2020. It has since appreciated in value to $315,000.

Here's how it performed with her last renter:

Monthly Rent	$2,045
Vacancy Loss	$102
Opex + MTC	$614
NOI	$1,329
Loan	$625
Monthly Cash	$704
Annual CF	$8,446

Note: Net operating income = NOI.
If you have paid off your mortgage, that is the cashflow from the investment. In her case, she still had a mortgage, so the monthly cashflow was $700, or $8450/year.

That last renter didn't leave the property in good condition, so she's looking at another renovation, or just selling it. Let's analyze it, step by step. First, she has about $184,000 of equity.

Value of Unit	$315,000
Debt	$131,000
Equity	$184,000

She thinks she'll have about 2.5% annual appreciation in the future. Appreciation in most markets has been a lot higher than that over the past decade. We expect a "reversion to the mean", where we have several years of lower appreciation. We know her annual cashflow is $8,450 after the mortgage payment.

Equity	Appreciation	Cash Flow	Total Return	Total Return %
184,000	$7,875	$8,446	$16,321	8.9%
184,000	$7,875	$8,446	$16,321	8.9%
	2.5%	4.6%		

The likely appreciation is the value of the property, $315,000 multiplied by the expected 2.5% annual rate of appreciation, or $7,875. Her total return is the appreciation plus the cashflow, or

$16,321 per year. Since she has $184,000 of equity, that's an 8.9% annual return.

This simple calculation doesn't consider the small amount of principal being paid off on the loan each month, or the tax value of the depreciation write off. That makes the math much easier to follow, and for most investors, doesn't change the answer.

What will happen if she does nothing?

Her equity of $184,000 will not have any transaction costs (since she is not selling), and there is no capital gain tax bill. The entire amount grows by 8.9% per year. That's a $16,321 increase in year one, as we showed above. In the second year, it had a bigger gain of $17,769. This is compounding interest. You earn 8.9% return on the original equity AND the interest that is re-invested.

As Einstein reportedly said, compounding interest is the eighth wonder of the world. In ten years, that $184,000 grows to $430,000.

	Do Nothing
Equity from Old Rentals	$184,000
Transaction Costs	
Capital Gains Tax	-
Amount to Invest	$184,000
Annual Return	8.9%
Start Balance	$184,000
Gain Year 1	$16,321
Balance End Year 1	$200,321
Gain Year 2	$17,769
Balance End Year 2	$218,090
Balance End Year 3	$237,435
Balance End Year 4	$258,495
Balance End Year 5	**$281,424**
Gain Year 6	$24,963
Blanace End Year 6	$306,387
Blanance End Year 7	$333,564
Blanance End Year 8	$363,151
Blanance End Year 9	$395,363
Blanance End Year 10	**$430,433**

Stay the course, and the $184,000 of equity today grows to $430,000 in ten years. This is why real estate investing has created so many millionaires.

What if she is tired of being an active investor? She could sell it now that her tenant has moved out.

Value of Unit	$315,000
Debt	$131,000
Equity	$184,000

Multiplying the value of the unit, $315,000, by 6% for sales costs, gives an estimated $18,900 of fees. That would include real estate commissions, title fees, and local transaction fees. You'd need to adjust that for your market.

Equity in Current Rentals Before Sales Costs		$184,000
Sales Costs (Commission, Title, Inspection)	6%	$18,900
Equity Net of Sales Costs		$165,100

That would consume $18,900 of her equity, leaving $165,000 to invest.

I won't bother you with the math here, but she might have capital gains and depreciation recapture tax of $29,700 to pay. Her CPA, of course, would be the final authority on that.

Let's imagine she wants to be done with this problem property and invest the proceeds, after paying the tax, in a balanced fund of stocks and bonds. Historically, that has returned around 8.1%.

	Stock Market
Equity from Old Rentals	$184,000
Transaction Costs	($18,900)
Capital Gains Tax	($29,736)
Amount to Invest	$135,364
Annual Return	8.10%
Start Balance	$135,364
Gain Year 1	$10,964
Balance End Year 1	$146,328
Gain Year 2	$11,853
Balance End Year 2	$158,181
Balance End Year 3	$170,993
Balance End Year 4	$184,844
Balance End Year 5	**$199,816**
Gain Year 6	$16,185
Blanace End Year 6	$216,001
Blanance End Year 7	$233,497
Blanance End Year 8	$252,411
Blanance End Year 9	$272,856
Blanance End Year 10	**$294,957**

Her $184,000 of equity today would be $135,000 after the tax payment and the sales costs. That $135,000 grows to $295,000 over a decade. She'd make more keeping the property and dealing with the headaches. But the stocks and bonds are easy, and very liquid – she can access the funds any time she wants. That's not true with real estate, which usually is not liquid.

Another option is to sell and invest in our Medium Term Income fund (MTI), which pays about 12%.

	MTI Fund
Equity from Old Rentals	$184,000
Transaction Costs	($18,900)
Capital Gains Tax	($29,736)
Amount to Invest	$135,364
Annual Return	12%
Start Balance	$135,364
Gain Year 1	$16,244
Balance End Year 1	$151,607
Gain Year 2	$18,193
Balance End Year 2	$169,800
Balance End Year 3	$190,176
Balance End Year 4	$212,997
Balance End Year 5	**$238,557**
Gain Year 6	$28,627
Blanace End Year 6	$267,184
Blanance End Year 7	$299,246
Blanance End Year 8	$335,156
Blanance End Year 9	$375,374
Blanance End Year 10	**$420,419**

You can see that after paying the taxes and transaction costs, the nest egg grows to $420,00 over a decade. This is just $10,000 short of the wealth creation if she kept the investment. This is passive and generates reliable quarterly cash she can use for living expenses.

A final option is to sell and invest for the long term in the National Diversified Fund (NDF), which targets 17-20% annualized returns after expenses. A nice feature is that we have two share classes for NDF.

- One share class has a slightly higher preferred return but does not give any depreciation. This tends to be a great choice if you are investing in your IRA or are investing with cash, and you don't need passive losses (check with your CPA to see what's best for your situation).

- The other share class has a slightly lower preferred return and gets all the depreciation.

	NDF8	Do Nothing
Equity from Old Rentals	$184,000	$184,000
Transaction Costs	($18,900)	
Capital Gains Tax	($15,207)	-
Amount to Invest	$149,893	$184,000
Annual Return	17%	8.9%
Start Balance	$149,893	$184,000
Gain Year 1	$25,482	$16,321
Balance End Year 1	$175,374	$200,321
Gain Year 2	$29,814	$17,769
Balance End Year 2	$205,188	$218,090
Balance End Year 3	$240,070	$237,435
Balance End Year 4	$280,882	$258,495
Balance End Year 5	**$328,632**	**$281,424**
Gain Year 6	$55,867	$24,963
Blanace End Year 6	$384,499	$306,387
Blanace End Year 7	$449,864	$333,564
Blanace End Year 8	$526,341	$363,151
Blanace End Year 9	$615,818	$395,363
Blanance End Year 10	**$720,508**	**$430,433**

If you get the depreciation shares, it can usually be used (check with your CPA) to offset some or all your capital gains from the sale of your investment property. In this case, it cut the tax nearly in half, from $29,700 to $15,200. The remaining equity grows over the next decade to $720,500.

In this situation, she can get out of the headaches of active management, manage her tax liability, and enjoy an entire passive investment that generates a much higher return over time.

What's the bottom line of these scenarios?

Do nothing and sell in 10 years	$246,000
Sell and Invest in MTI	$285,000
Sell and Invest in NDF	$568,000

*****

Would you like to see what these options could look like for your portfolio? Go to http://irontoncapital.com/gopassive to choose your best time for your free portfolio review so you can get all the information to take to your financial advisors.

How to optimize your IRA

What if you have a rollover 401K from an old employer, and/or a self-directed IRA? It's probably invested in the stock and bond market now, getting (historically) a return of around 7-8% per year.

You can move this to a self-directed IRA custodian, and then your menu of investing choices will be much broader than the mutual funds you likely have available to you now. You could invest, for example, in our MTI or NDF funds.

One amazing concept is to invest in NDF, or a similar private equity fund that isn't liquid (e.g., you cannot sell shares in a market like you can for a mutual fund) and you don't have decision rights. You can engage a specialized CPA to do a Fair Market Value (FMV) assessment of your investment. In most cases, since the investment is not liquid, and you do not have decision rights, the FMV could be less than the original amount of your investment.

You can give the CPA's FMV analysis to your IRA custodian, and they will reduce the market value (on paper – in reality, the value does not change, of course) of your IRA as a result.

You can then convert your traditional IRA to a Roth IRA. You will, of course, pay the taxes on the value of the investment, which is now considerably less, thanks to the FMV study. As with any other Roth IRA, it will now grow tax free.

The after-tax savings can be considerable.

To see this more in-depth, get our free training on How to Optimize Your IRA for a Big Tax savings at https://irontoncapital.com/bigirasavings and then talk to your CPA to see if this tax strategy is right for you.

What is the role of depreciation and my taxes?

We've mentioned several times the power of depreciation, and you might have already heard of depreciation, so how does it work with real estate and your taxes?

Depreciation in real estate is a way to account for the wear and tear on buildings or properties over time. Just like cars lose value as they age, so do buildings. Even if a building is still in good shape, the IRS considers it less valuable as it gets older (even though, in reality, it's probably appreciating in value).

Depreciation allows property owners to deduct a portion of the property's value from their taxes each year. This deduction helps offset the costs of owning and maintaining the property. However, it's important to follow specific rules and guidelines set by the government to ensure accurate depreciation calculations.

Overall, depreciation is a useful tool for property owners to manage their tax liabilities and expenses related to property ownership. And that's why we focus on leveraging depreciation in our Class B shares in our National Diversified Fund (NDF).

*****

To explore if you could leverage depreciation with our NDF, go to http://irontoncapital.com/gopassive to choose your best time for your free portfolio review so you can get all the information to take to your financial advisors.

Where to park your cash?

Finally, many people keep six to twelve months of living expenses in their emergency reserve fund. Often, that is parked at a local bank earning a minimal interest rate, or in a money market account making not much more. Instead, our investors asked us to create our Short Term Income fund (STI) to make around 8-9%, with quarterly dividend payments.

Pretax return	3%	8%
Marginal income tax	39%	23%
Aftertax return	1.83%	6.16%
Year 0	$100,000	$100,000
Year 1	$101,830	$106,160
Year 2	$103,693	$112,699
Year 3	$105,591	$119,642
Year 4	$107,523	$127,012
Year 5	$109,491	$134,836
Year 6	$111,495	$143,141
Year 7	$113,535	$151,959
Year 8	$115,613	$161,320
Year 9	$117,729	$171,257
Year 10	$119,883	$181,806
Aftertax STI-Bank spread		$61,923

Plus, most of the STI dividends are taxed as a REIT (real estate investment trust). For most investors, the REIT tax rate is less than their marginal ordinary income rate (that you pay on bank interest, for example). This can save quite a bit on your tax bill. As always, check with your CPA.

For example, many of our investors like to keep three months' income in the bank and the rest in STI, where they can get the money out with 30 days' notice. If starting with $100,000, over a decade you could generate an additional $62,000 after tax.

As always, these are illustrations of returns and actual investment performance can and will vary, as always, speak to your CPA.

*****

To ask how our income funds may put your money to work harder for you, go to http://irontoncapital.com/gopassive to choose your best time to talk to our Investor Relations team so you can get all the information to take to your financial advisors.

How to stay on top of the real estate trends?

Finally, one of the most important things you can do as an investor…whether you are in stocks, bonds, or real estate…either active or passive…is stay on top of the economic trends. This tends to separate the lower and higher performance investors.

We do monthly updates for our investing family on economic and markets trends and how they shape our thinking for real estate investment strategy.

If you would like to attend, you can sign up for our next live update at https://irontoncapital.com/marketupdates

Chapter 5: Getting Started

Now that you know a lot more about passive, diversified real estate investment and how it could fit in your overall financial plan, let's review how to get started.

Pre-Planning Activities

As they say in woodworking: measure twice, cut once. It is important to plan before you act.

Activities within the **family**.
- ✓ Decide if real estate investment is right for your portfolio.
  - o See Chapter 1 of this book.
- ✓ Decide if you want to invest passively or actively.
  - o See Appendix 3 of this book.

Activities with your **advisors**.
Talk to your advisory team – most importantly your CPA, but also your attorney and financial advisor if you have them.

- ✓ CPA:
  - o Tax considerations.
  - o For example, if you have the option to get more passive losses through depreciation, how much would you want?
- ✓ CPA or financial advisor.
  - o For example, which investments should be purchased with cash, versus through your self-directed IRA?
  - o Does it matter if you personally own the investment, or is there a tax benefit to another method?
- ✓ Attorney:
  - o How to hold title (for example, in concert with the rest of your estate plan).
  - o Detailed review of specific fund documents when you are about to invest.

Activities with potential Fund **General Partners** and/or Sponsors.
- ✓ See how their fund(s) fit your requirements.

Due Diligence - 8 Considerations

I always consider eight factors as I'm planning my investments:

1. Ask about the **tax** implications of real estate investments, including deductions, depreciation, and potential capital gains taxes.
2. Discuss the investment's **alignment** with your financial goals and risk tolerance.
3. Ask about the **expected returns**, including both income and appreciation potential, as well as any associated fees or expenses.
4. Ask about their **track record** with similar investments.
5. Inquire about the investment's **liquidity** and exit strategies in case you need to sell your stake.
6. Seek clarification on the **due diligence** process, including property evaluations and management procedures, to ensure the investment aligns with your overall financial plan and objectives.
7. Finally, when it is time to make the investment, check with your advisors on how to **hold title**.
8. **Fund** the investment.

Let's spend a moment exploring each facet of the pre-planning and due diligence process.

1. Tax. Real estate investments come with various tax implications that can impact your financial outcomes.

- **Deductions** such as mortgage interest, property taxes, and operating expenses can help reduce taxable income from real estate investments.
- **Depreciation** allows you to deduct a portion of the property's cost each year to reflect its wear and tear, lowering your taxable income further.
- Additionally, when you sell a property, you may be subject to **capital gains taxes** on any profits earned.

- However, certain **tax strategies**, such as like-kind (e.g., "1031") exchanges or investing through tax-advantaged accounts, can help mitigate capital gains taxes.

Understanding these tax implications and seeking guidance from a CPA or financial advisor can optimize your tax efficiency and overall investment returns in real estate.

For Example, at Ironton Capital:
- The National Diversified Fund (NDF) will have an option to generate depreciation you can use to offset your capital gains and/or passive losses with other investments.
- The Short Term Income Fund (STI) is taxed as a REIT (Real Estate Investment Trust). For most investors, that is a lower tax bracket than their marginal ordinary income rate.
- Choose your time at http://irontoncapital.com/gopassive to learn more about how our funds might help with your situation.

Only you can decide, but usually the CPA is the better resource. Many financial advisors have deep training and extensive experience with stocks and bonds, but very little exposure to real estate. As a result, they often will be reluctant to offer much advice on real estate. Since they don't have much exposure to real estate, real estate advice may be seen as a higher risk to them, so this set of activities is led nearly exclusively by the passive investor.

2. Alignment. When considering an investment's alignment with your financial goals and risk tolerance, it's essential to assess how it fits into your overall financial plan and creates generational wealth.
- Evaluate whether the investment helps you **achieve specific objectives**, such as building wealth, generating passive income, or diversifying your portfolio.
- Consider your **risk tolerance**, or how comfortable you are with potential fluctuations in the investment's value.

- Higher-risk investments may offer the potential for greater returns, but also come with increased uncertainty and volatility.
- Conversely, lower-risk investments may provide more stability but offer lower potential returns.

For Example, at Ironton Capital:

- The National Diversified Fund (NDF) will have dozens of properties in a diverse portfolio. As a result, it'll be lower risk, but have less opportunity to achieve above (or below) its 17-20% annual target return. Of course, prior performance is not a predictor of future performance.
- Ironton periodically offers single-investment, focused funds. Due to the lack of diversification, we'd expect more volatile returns. It is like selecting a single stock vs. a mutual fund.
- Ironton's income funds like Short Term Income (STI) and Medium Term Income (MTI) are based on hundreds (or more) of small debt instruments, which really diversifies risk.
- Consult with your financial advisors as you evaluate options from us or other private equity funds.
- Choose your time at http://irontoncapital.com/gopassive to learn more about how our funds might help with your situation.

By aligning the investment with your financial goals and risk tolerance, you can make decisions that suit your individual circumstances and aspirations while balancing potential rewards and risks.

This set of activities is mostly led by the passive investor. The Sponsor or GP (General Partner) will be able to provide some input to you and your advisory team.

3. Returns. When inquiring about expected returns for a real estate investment, it's crucial to consider both income and appreciation potential.

- **Income** refers to the regular cashflow generated from the investment, such as rental payments from tenants.
- Understanding the expected rental income helps assess the investment's ability to generate ongoing returns.
- **Appreciation potential** refers to the property's expected increase in value over time. This could come from factors like improvements to the property or overall market trends.
- Additionally, inquire about any **associated fees or expenses**, such as property management fees, maintenance costs, or administrative expenses.

Understanding these costs allows you to evaluate the investment's overall profitability and ensure it aligns with your financial goals.

For Example, at Ironton Capital:
- NDF is designed to have minimal income and have most of the returns characterized as long-term capital gains. NDF is not liquid and requires a 4–6-year commitment.
- STI is designed to have maximum liquidity and has tax-preferred treatment as a REIT. Principal preservation is a high priority. As a result, it has lower returns in the 8-9% range with predictable quarterly dividends.
- MTI has an intermediate level of liquidity, and accordingly, an intermediate level of returns. The target is 11-13% annually, paid in equal quarterly installments.
- All these return projections are net of all fees.

This set of activities is initiated by the Sponsor or the GP. They should have a very detailed business case, examining several economic scenarios. If not, that is a red flag. If you have the business skills, time, and interest, ask for a copy of the XLS (Microsoft Excel) model. If you lack the skills and you have a family member or business associate you trust that loves Excel, consider enlisting such help.

Ironton Capital always welcomes the opportunity to educate our prospective investors on our business analysis models. The more we can teach you, the more comfortable you will be, and that's what you should expect from your GPs.

Ask the Sponsor to show you the high points of the model and how it works. Which variables have the most impact on the profit? For developing a new apartment complex, you might find these variables are most impactful:

- Rents and occupancy rates upon completion
- Finishing on time and on budget
- The assumptions for the sales price when complete and stabilized

Ask the Sponsor to share the research they used to guide the assumptions in the model.

For example:
- What rents are **comparable** existing apartment complexes near the new project getting? How do the amenities and features of our project compare? Since yours will be new and shiny, your project will usually outperform similar but dated properties nearby.
- What is the Sponsor's **track record** for construction management on prior projects with a similar scope? Is there a fixed cost bid for the construction? Does this local government have a good reputation for being business friendly and expediting the permitting and construction approval process?
- What **recent prices** have sales of similar projects achieved in the market? Are the assumptions of the sale reasonable in comparison?

Ask how the Sponsor/GP has managed these key variables in the past. This isn't nosy or "bad behavior" on your part. <u>A good Sponsor will welcome these questions from a passive investor</u>. If you are curious, explore this in depth. If you have the passion for this, this will be the most time-consuming element for you. If you are not that curious, it's ok to review this at a high level if you otherwise feel comfortable with the Sponsor.

4. Track Record. Be sure to ask about the track record of prior investments. This isn't as easy as asking a public stock mutual fund manager about their history, however. A private equity fund manager may be reluctant to share their track record of performance for several reasons.

- One primary concern is confidentiality and competitive advantage. Sharing detailed performance data could reveal proprietary investment strategies, deal flow, or other sensitive information that the manager prefers to keep private to maintain a competitive edge in the market.
- Often, a large part of the outperformance is that the GP has negotiated private favorable economics with the Sponsors they invest in. There are strict non-disclosure agreements (NDA) surrounding these arrangements.
- Of course, if the fund's performance has been subpar or inconsistent, the manager may be hesitant to disclose this information to potential investors, as it could negatively impact fundraising efforts or reputation.
- Furthermore, regulatory restrictions or compliance concerns may limit the manager's ability to share performance data, particularly if it includes sensitive financial information or conflicts with securities laws.

Overall, the decision to share track records of performance is complex and may involve weighing confidentiality, competitiveness, regulatory compliance, and investor relations considerations. Don't be surprised if it's much more difficult to get track record information from some than you'd expect.

On Request, Ironton is happy to discuss prior performance as part of a potential investor's due diligence process. If you would like to learn more, go to http://irontoncapital.com/gopassive to choose your best time to talk with our team.

5. Liquidity. When asking about an investment's liquidity and exit strategies, it's important to understand how easy it would be to convert your investment into cash if needed.

- **Liquidity** refers to how quickly and easily you can sell your stake in an investment and access your money.
- Real estate investments are typically MUCH less liquid than stocks or bonds, as selling a property can take time and may be subject to market conditions.
- Inquire about **potential exit strategies**, such as selling the property, refinancing, or participating in a buyout agreement.

Understanding these options allows you to plan for potential financial needs or changes in circumstances and ensures that your investment remains flexible and aligned with your overall financial strategy.

Ask the Sponsor or GP about the liquidity options, if any, for the investment you are considering. Many passive real estate investments will require 4-6 years of commitment with no liquidity. This is what you give up earning up to twice the return you would get in the stock market!

6. Due Diligence. Inquiring about the due diligence process is crucial before investing in real estate.

- Thoroughly **evaluate** the property and its management procedures to ensure it meets your investment criteria.
- **Property evaluations** assess factors like location, condition, and potential for rental income or appreciation.
- Understanding the **management procedures** involves knowing how the property will be operated and maintained, including tenant management, maintenance schedules, and financial reporting.
- How these aspects will be handled and what **safeguards** are in place to protect your investment.

Conducting thorough due diligence helps mitigate risks and ensures that the investment aligns with your financial goals and expectations.

If you pursue the Syndication option, you will select projects and their Sponsors directly. This is likely building a portfolio of individual stocks based on your own research. In this case, you will have considerable research to do here.

If you pursue the Private Equity fund option, you just need to trust the General Partners of the fund and their strategy. You are then delegating to the GP to research each individual Sponsor and project. This is like investing in a mutual fund to save yourself the headache of research.

Ironton shares extensive details of our due diligence process with our investors as they narrow down their choices of which fund(s) are best for their needs.

7. Hold Title: Talk to your attorney and cpa, they can guide you through this process. For example, you can hold it in your name or jointly with your spouse. You may discover, through estate planning, it makes sense to develop a trust to hold these investments. These are just some possibilities. Your attorney, cpa or financial planner may have other suggestions.

Ask the GP in the Fund if you are allowed to change how you hold title if your estate planning needs evolve over time.

For example, Ironton has flexibility to change how you hold title, and most General Partners should have the ability.

8. **Fund** the investment. If you are investing with cash, this is as simple as wiring the funds to the General Partner.

If you are using a self-directed IRA, you need to have a self-directed custodian that supports working with real estate investments. Most do not! You can ask the GP of your fund, or your CPA, for recommendations.

Be aware that moving funds from your traditional IRA (such as Schwab, Fidelity, or Vanguard) to your self-directed custodian could take a few weeks. Once your funds are transferred, the new custodian might require a week (or more) to make the investment, once you provide the "Direction of Investment" paperwork. As you are interviewing different service providers, ask them about this. Usually they can move faster, but they may charge expedite fees to do so.

Next Steps?

Real estate investing is my passion. Every day, I still dive into active and passive investing, but not everyone has the time or passion for real estate that I do. I believe that everyone should have access to this vehicle for growing their financial freedom.

You have now learned what I consider to be the most essential elements to passive investing while closely managing your risk. Now it's time for you to take the next step and get started talking to your family and advisors. Decide on where you want to go, your risk tolerance to get there, and then plan the vehicles for wealth that are right for you.

If Ironton Capital can be of service to you for your journey, then reach out to us at https://irontoncapital.com/gopassive and let's talk about how our passive funds could fit into your portfolio.

Ironton Capital Funds

Ironton Capital is a multi-strategy real estate private equity firm. We provide tailored solutions to investors with short- and long-term products.

Investor benefits:
- Diversification
- Principal protection focus
- Tax optimization
- Passive losses for investors that desire them
- Liquidity in our income funds

Because not every investor has the same needs, we offer multiple paths for passive investing.

	National Diversified Funds (NDFs)	Short Term Income Funds (STIs)	Medium Term Income Funds (MTIs)
Sector	Real Estate	Real Estate ~80% Medical Receivables ~20%	Real Estate
Target Returns	17%+ 5-6 year timeline	8-9%	11-13% fixed based on AUM
Liquidity	Cash distributed as individual projects cash flow.	Quarterly dividends. Principal back with 30 day notice.	Quarterly dividends. Access to principal after one year lockup.
Fund Size	$10-20M	$200M+	$30M+
Individual Investments	10-15	200-400	25K+
Tax Advantages	Targeting depreciation tax shelter	REIT income treatment	No tax advantage

Download this overview at https://irontoncapital.com/icoverview

National Diversified Funds (NDFs)

Our flagship Growth Fund is a great option for investors that don't need income today; they're looking for just more equity appreciation than they have now. It helps you achieve diversification without the need for active portfolio management with a target IRR of 17-21%.

Of course, past returns don't predict future results. Consult with your financial advisors. This is not an offer to invest; contact us for subscription information with all of the details.

- Must be an accredited investor.
- Targeted Internal Rate of Return (IRR) of 17-20%+ (net of fees) to investors.
- Diversified across Strategy, Sponsor, Asset Class and Geography (The 4 Pillars of Diversification!).
- Because this is a fund of funds, you get exposure to 30-40 individual commercial properties with one simple investment.
- Often includes apartments, across various states, managed by institutional-level managers.
- No Liquidity.
- 4-6 year target hold period.
- Most returns taxed as capital gains.
- 2 Class Shares
  - Class A higher rate of preferred income, no depreciation.
  - Class B lower rate of preferred income, depreciation class shares offer 20-40% passive losses in year one if needed.

Short Term Income Funds (STIs)

Our Short Term Income Fund (STI) is a great opportunity for our investors to have a short-term or rainy day cash reserve option with returns higher than money market accounts.

- Must be an accredited investor.
- Targeted 8-9% annual return.
- Makeup 80% hard money lending to real estate investors focused on loans in Denver and Salt Lake City for residential and commercial.
- First deed of trust – highly secure.
- Average loan to value on each of these loans is about 60-65% and our group is very conservative in their underwriting.
- 250+ loans in portfolio provides diversification.
- Other 20% in medical account receivables.
- Liquid on 30 days notice, 1% fee on what you take out if under a year.
- Annual Asset Management Fee 2%.
- Quarterly dividends of about 2% with an annual return of about 8-9% per year.

Medium Term Income Funds (MTIs)

Our Medium Term Income Fund (MTI) provides investors with a targeted 11-13% annual return compared to CDs, depending on assets invested with Ironton Capital, only varies with assets under management (AUM) underlying is fixed. Dividends paid quarterly with some liquidity given advance notice.

Great option for investors wanting further diversification that is completely uncorrelated with real estate or the stock market.

- Must be an accredited investor.
- Provides financial solutions to Medical Service Providers.
- Advancing funds against outstanding medical receivables via Letters of Credit.
- These outstanding funds are paid by insurance for claims, not individuals.
- Purchasing receivables at a discount under Letters of Protection.
- Diversified across 25,000+ individual medical invoices.
- Investors can expect a targeted fixed return of between 11-13% per year based on assets under management.
- Quarterly dividends of about 3% per quarter of your investment, beginning from the first full quarter post-investment.
- 8-10-year target hold period. Most returns taxed as capital gains, open-ended 10-year lock, amortization at 7 years, will make interest only payments until 7 years.
- Fund has a 1-year lockup period, after which investors can request redemptions quarterly.
- No upfront fees. Fees come on the backend, and it's basically just a small percentage (less than 2%) between what we make and what we pay our limited partners.

Download this overview at https://irontoncapital.com/icoverview

Appendix 1: How Real Estate Professionals Can Use This Book

If you work with investors, you are likely often asked about the viability, in the current market conditions, to purchase additional real estate investment property.

Appendix 3 should help with **new investors**. It's a great way to provide a structured educational and decision process for what they should buy, and what investment skills they should be working on.

Some of these potential buyers are not sure if they should be active or passive investors. Appendix 3 should help them sort this out rapidly. This should help you avoid allocating a lot of time in a prospect that really shouldn't buy investment real estate.

For your **established investors**, you likely are being asked if now is a good time to sell…and if so, what they should use the proceeds to invest in.

Some of your clients are still enjoying being active investors. If your local market conditions are favorable, Appendix 3 should also help you to help these clients determine what exactly to buy next.

Some of your clients are less excited about being active investors anymore, even if they have a property management company helping them. They want to sell, which is a potential listing for you. They are not sure what they should do next. Almost universally, they are not excited about the prospect of paying taxes.

Chapter 4 has a section that outlines how these clients can sell, not do a 1031 exchange, and get off the active investor treadmill. It outlines tax management strategies and makes the business case that even if a reduced tax bill must be paid, often in the long run, the investor is much better off.

Another common strategy for active investors selling a real estate investment is to roll the proceeds into a DST.

Understanding the DST, Delaware Statutory Trust

A Delaware Statutory Trust (DST) is a legal entity used in real estate investment that allows multiple investors to own a beneficial interest in a property. DSTs are commonly used in 1031 exchanges, where investors can defer capital gains taxes by exchanging one investment property for another. In a DST, a trustee manages the property on behalf of the investors, who receive income distributions based on their ownership percentage.

DSTs offer passive investment opportunities with potential tax benefits and diversification, making them popular among investors seeking real estate exposure without the responsibilities of property management.

The problem is that they have high expenses and usually have low returns. That might make your client less excited about selling now.

Appendix 2 will help provide you with information about how your client can exit their investment, and why a DST often is not the best option. By showing better outcomes, you can often position your client for success by selling now, and not using a DST.

We are happy to be a resource for you and your clients. We can set up a conference call with you and your clients, so they will have the investment facts they need to make a well-informed business decision. In most cases, listing the property to sell it and move on is the optimal answer. Simply book your time with our team at http://irontoncapital.com/gopassive

Appendix 2: When is a DST Not the Best Choice for a 1031 Exchange?

I'm frequently asked by investors if they should sell their current rental properties. There are a lot of factors that go into the decision. The most important is, are you still enjoying owning and running it? (Running it might be a limited scope of work with a great property manager that you trust).

If you have ten properties, you likely have one that just always seems to have maintenance problems or attracts problem tenants. Regardless of the economics, that's probably the one you should dispose of first. Your spouse with thank you!

Alternatively, you might be less fascinated with tenant requests than you were in the beginning, and you're daydreaming about TRUE passive income, vs. being an active landlord. Even if you have a property manager, there are still plenty of decisions to make and headaches to manage.

Once you decide to sell a property, you can talk to your CPA to find out what the tax impact will be. You'll have some capital gains (generally your net proceeds after sales costs, less your purchase price, less any renovation work). And you'll have something mysteriously called "depreciation recapture."

You can depreciate part of your property each year, and it can shield you from the tax liability from the cashflow your rental(s) generated. You can think of this as an interest-free loan from the IRS. Even though you never wrote a check to anyone for this depreciation, the IRS let you reduce your income each year...savings you some tax. When you sell, you have to pay this back.

Your total tax liability when you sell is both the capital gain and the depreciation recapture. You can legally postpone the payment of both if you do a 1031 exchange. The 1031 name comes from the section of the tax code where Congress set out the rules of how it works.

The paperwork is not hard to do. Finding a replacement property you like is by far the most important and difficult task.

If you don't find a replacement property, or if you want to become a truly passive investor, the idea of buying a larger replacement property may not be exciting to you (and your family). If so, your options are to:
1. Use a 1031 exchange and invest in a DST.
2. Pay the tax and use the money for anything you want.
3. Invest in something that will defer some/all your gains without a 1031 exchange.

Let's explore your options one by one.

OPTION 1 – DST
The Delaware Statutory Trust (DST) will work with most 1031 exchanges. The benefits are you can defer the payment of your capital gains tax. The downside is there are a lot of fees and expenses, and there is a limited selection of investments that are configured as a DST. Getting out of a DST can be difficult. Finally, most DSTs invest with limited (or no) leverage in very, very conservative investments. For example, the DST might purchase a Home Depot. It's leased to a great company, but the return on investment will be low, and the annual rent increases are usually very small in retail triple-net properties like this. You might make 5-9% year, overall.

OPTION 2 – SELL AND PAY TAX

While it seems very counterintuitive, over a ten-year period, most investors will come out ahead by investing in a truly passive real estate investment that delivers 17-20% a year AFTER tax, vs. investing in a DST that pays 5-9% per year WITHOUT tax. Ironton Capital offers several funds that offer returns in this range. They are all entirely passive, so it's effortless for you.

OPTION 3 – SELL, DEFER SOME / ALL TAX

Our National Diversified Fund (NDF) has two share classes to address the needs of two of our different types of investors. Class A shares get a slightly higher preferred return but does not get any depreciation. This works well for IRA investors, for example. The other share type, Class B, gets a slightly lower preferred return but gets ALL the depreciation.

Let's imagine the NDF fund buys an older apartment building at a discount that needs a lot of work. The rents are $500/month below market. We'll renovate the building, raise the rents, then sell it.

Purchase Price	$4,000,000
Debt	$3,000,000
Equity	$1,000,000
Class A: High Preference, No Depreciation	$500,000
Class B: Low Preference, All Depreciation	$500,000

Without anything special, for residential property, you can write of the improvements (not the land) over 27.5 years.

Here's how that tax write-off calculation would work:

Ordinary Situation	
Value of Land	$750,000
Value of Improvements	$3,250,000
Depreciation Life (Years)	27.5
Annual Depreciation Writeoff	$118,182
Class B Shares:	$500,000
% of Initial Investment Written Of	24%

24% of your investment in Class B shares would be written off each year (talk to your CPA for your unique situation). This can offset some/most of your capital gain from the sale of your old rental.

But we can do even better.

Usually about 50% of a NDF fund is a remodel of old assets that need a full remodel (the other half invests in new development, which doesn't generate depreciation for a few years). We hire a specialized accounting firm to do a cost segregation study. Normally, the CPA will say the entire value of the apartment is $4,000,000, the land is $750,000, and we'll just assume we write off all $3,250,000 of improvements over 27.5 years, or $118,000 per year.

In the segregation study, the CPA breaks the $3,250,000 into many categories. For example, $300,000 might be assigned to the roof, which is in poor condition and only has a three-year life. We can accelerate the depreciation for this part of the building. Similarly, some value is assigned to kitchens, baths, paint, and carpet, which might all be torn out and fully replaced as part of the remodel plan. Rather than those assets being written off over 27.5 years, they can be written off much faster.

Let's imagine that the study finds that 5% of the value (usually its higher) can be written off immediately. Here's how things change for the first year write off:

Accelerated Situation	
Cost Segregation Study	
% of Asset That Can Be Written Off ASAP	5%
$ of Asset That Can Be Written Off ASAP	$200,000
Normal Annual Write Off	$118,182
Total Year 1 Write Off	$318,182
Class B Shares:	$500,000
% of Initial Investment Written Off	64%

Now the $500,000 investment in the class B depreciation shares gets $318,000 of write off in year 1. Again, talk to your CPA for your situation, but often this may be sufficient to offset most or all your gain when you sell the old property. You can win by getting a truly passive investment and win by legally deferring your taxes, too.

*****

And if Ironton Capital can be of service to you sorting out these 3 paths, then reach out to us at https://irontoncapital.com/gopassive and choose your best time to talk.

Your CPA is welcome to be on the call. Our goal is to give you all the facts and alternatives so you and your family can make a fully informed business decision about how to process your rental. Financial freedom through passive investing is much closer than you think.

Appendix 3: Is Active Real Estate Investing Right for Me?

You hear about active real estate investing as a vehicle to wealth all around you, in the media, from your financial advisors and even your neighbors, but is active real estate investing right for you?

I have written several books on active real estate investing and I've pulled out this summary of each active investment category for you. It shows you exactly what it takes to potentially make a profit with each investment approach to give you an insider's look into the industry.

To get a sense of which categories are best for your skills and personality, the second half of this appendix will have some questions to help you evaluate your skills. Many of the categories will not be a good fit for some investors, so this can help you save a lot of time.

Executive Summary of Real Estate Investment Categories:

- A summary of the categories of real estate investing. Each category is explored in much more depth in its individual chapter.
- Next, we review the skills, time, and monetary resources that you can devote to your real estate investments – this is "what you give."
- Finally, we make some recommendations of which types of investments you might wish to consider, given your unique situation.

Types of Active Investments.

Assignments. If you don't have much equity (e.g., cash to use as a down payment), and/or if your credit power is limited, assignments can be a way to get started in real estate investing. You will need to have a strong "sales" personality to succeed at it, though.

Rental Condo or Rental Home. This is the purchase of a residential property to be rented out to tenants, usually on a 6–12-month lease term. This is how most new landlords get started. You may hire out all the property management functions, but in many cases, you will do many of them on your own. There are smaller down payment requirements for homes and condos than for larger rental buildings. The purchase process and financing process is very similar to what you experienced buying the home you live in now. It's a great way for beginners to get started.

Small Apartment Building (2-4 units) to be rented to tenants, usually for 12-month terms. This is often what the rental condo or home landlords "graduate" to. In some markets they cost a little more than a rental home but are much more likely to generate positive cashflow. This results in less cashflow risk; if one unit is empty, you have other tenants that still help you with the mortgage payment, so it doesn't all come out of your pocket. Many owners will start to delegate some of the property management tasks to an on-site assistant (typically the most responsible tenant), such as yard maintenance and showing empty units. The financing process is only slightly more involved than a residential loan. The purchase process is also very similar to purchasing a home. It is also a good way for beginners to get started.

Large Apartment Building (5 and more units). With five units and up you are still targeting tenants for 12 months at a time (buildings with more than five units are considered "commercial" property). The loans are somewhat more difficult to qualify for, and usually a larger down payment percentage is needed. Large apartment buildings are a less frequent choice for the new investor; this is usually what landlords with several years of experience "trade up" to. That said, we have had newbie landlords purchase 12-unit buildings and do very well. Cashflows on larger buildings are more stable than for smaller buildings, and the economies of scale make it practical (and desirable) to hire a property manager to take over most of the work for you. This reduces the hassle factor of the landlord process dramatically. If you are a busy professional that doesn't need another hobby, this might be a good fit.

Fix and Flips involve purchasing a property that needs work. The scope can range from the basic "paint and carpet", to extensive overhauls, to scraping a decrepit property and completely starting over. It usually does not involve tenants, and the objective is to get in and out of the property as quickly as possible. Great for beginners with the right skill set or the willingness to learn.

Conversion of Apartments into Condos are a synthesis of the fix and flip and rental operations – purchasing an apartment building in a neighborhood dominated by owner occupants, then converting the building from apartment building to condominium. Usually requires renovation of the units to meet the expectations of owner-occupant buyers in that area. Though complex and time consuming, condo conversions have wonderful tax advantages compared to fix and flips and often have superior returns to all other asset classes. Ideally suited for the sophisticated investor with extensive experience.

You need to be in the right phase of a market cycle for this to work. At the time of this writing, in most parts of the US, it's not the right time. It can be the right time if the apartment cost/SF (square foot) is at least $100 - $150 LESS than the price of a nice condo/ SF. Now, at least in Denver, apartments cost more $/SF than condos, so we're a long way from this strategy being viable. That will change – it always does.

Scrapes, Pops and New Construction involve purchasing a small home in an expensive neighborhood that may or may not need work. The home is bulldozed, and a new home or duplex is put on the lot.

Alternatively, the existing home is renovated, and more square footage is added on. A pop-top is adding a second story to an existing home to add more square footage (commonly, a master bedroom suite). The investor that succeeds in this segment usually has quite a lot of real estate experience.

Passive Real Estate Investing. If none of this sounds appealing, the beginning part of this book is for you. Let someone who is full-time and experienced do the work, and just share some of the profits when the project is successful.

Assessing Your Skills and Resources

Let's evaluate where you are now, and what you like to do, with eight criteria. Let's begin by reviewing what the typical requirements are for successful investing in each investment category. You can compare those requirements to the self-assessment that you complete here to get an idea of how appropriate the investment class is for your current situation. This takes time and effort. Trust me, it's worth it. We've seen hundreds of clients learn critical aspects of themselves and their investing potential by evaluating these criteria.

Equity Needed is how many liquid assets you and/or your investment team will need to have. Purchasing an apartment building, for example, usually requires at least 20% down on a purchase price that might start at $500,000, depending on the market. Realistically in Denver, you'd pay $150,000 - $200,000 per door, so a 12 unit might cost over $2 million. 25-30% is not uncommon for a downpayment. You would need $100,000 in cash just to get into the game for smaller rentals and $600,000+ for the twelve-unit building.

Credit Score will be important for some types of investments. Large apartment loans require nearly impeccable credit for the best terms. A small rental or fix and flip might require solid, though not perfect, credit. If you can put down 20%, you can often purchase a small rental even if your credit is far less than perfect. In general,

- If your credit score is under 620, you have poor credit.
- From 620 to 680 is average, and
- Above 680 would be good.
- 740 and above is great!

We'll discuss the breakpoints for excellent, average, and poor credit in the "Where the Pros Get the Money" chapter and provide suggestions of how to improve your score.

Experience with Contractors will make some types of projects more pleasant. Fix and flips, as a category, benefit the most from this type of experience. We did not have much experience when we undertook our first projects and we still managed to muddle through (but we learned a lot on our first projects and made lots of mistakes). We have worked with many investors with the same experience. On the other hand, if you purchase a larger apartment building that already has a competent property manager in place, you will need less experience with contractors.

Experience with Property Managers makes purchasing a rental property easier. It certainly is not essential, and you can learn by doing. We'll outline the advantages and disadvantages in the rental chapters.

Time Required Each Week varies on the project specifics, but we'll make some broad generalizations, so you have a sense of the level of commitment you'll have to make to improve your chances of success.

The Number of Monthly Interactions (e.g., how many times you visit the property or get phone calls about it) is also important to some people. They are happy spending one or two long sessions on the property but would be highly annoyed to have twenty very short interactions. Others, due to personal commitments, might have the opposite preference. We'll help set your expectations.

Perception of Hassle varies as much by individual as it does by project, but again, we can offer some broad guidelines.

Risk Tolerance is the level of comfort that you and the key people that influence your decisions have with risk and ambiguity. If you are going to be awake at 3AM every morning worrying about this decision it may not be the right asset category for you.

Reality Check

As you read through the criteria and how they vary among the different types of real estate investments, you'll detect a pattern of tradeoffs. For example, you can bring a lot of equity and a very strong credit score, and then purchase a large apartment building with a property manager – little effort is required on your part. Or…if you have no money and no credit, you will have to have a lot of time available and a high degree of willingness to accept hassles. There are, of course, a few options in the middle that require a degree of both. Finally, if you have great credit, lots of money, lots of skill, and lots of time to focus on the project, you are a developer – and you can focus on the very high return projects such as converting apartments to condos or scraping old buildings and putting up new ones in the most expensive neighborhoods.

Unlike late night TV infomercials, there are no reliable and ethical methods to make money with no risk, no credit, no cash, and no effort. They don't exist in the real world. Period. Anybody who tells you different is selling something. You'll have to bring something to the table to get a reward. Before people begin their career in real estate investing, they often think they need to have a lot of cash on hand to get started. The truth is, there are certain types of investments that will not require large sums of equity up-front.

As in anything in life, however, more cash does make things easier. Hopefully, as you progress in your investing career and build up your funds, additional investment opportunities will become available to you. The following chart will give you a summary of the equity requirements for different types of real estate investments. You can explore each type of investment in more detail in each of the following chapters.

Equity Needed

There are many potential sources for the funds. You could use your checking and savings accounts, take a loan out against your 401K, get a HELOC (home equity line of credit) if your residence has any equity, or borrow from friends and family members. We have seen clients take cash advances from their credit cards to get their funds. That is more aggressive than many investors might want to get, but it is an option. This is where evaluating your risk tolerance becomes critical.

Investment Type	Equity requirements
Assignments	**$0 may be possible, $10,000 – 20,000 is typical.** One of the appealing attributes of Assignments is you don't need much money or credit to play. The money is for the earnest money deposit. Alas, this tends to be the most competitive sector of real estate investing since the entry barriers are so low. You will hear about "how easy it is" from guys selling you $1,000 training packages. It's not easy at all.
Rental Condo Rental Home Small (2-4 unit) Apartment	**$25,000 and up.** 15-20% of the purchase price is generally required to be put down on the loan. Lenders will also require six months of operating expenses in reserves. For example, you might put 20% down on a $150k property and deposit $5k into your operating account. Three- and four-unit properties usually require 25%-30% down. Ex: Cos 1Br CND: $150K and 15% down + closing costs. Denver & Northern Co DSF: $300k and 20% down = $60k + closing costs.
Large (5+ unit) Apartment	**$150,000-$225,000 and up.** Buildings over four units require a commercial loan. Sometimes a lender will loan up to 80% of the purchase price, requiring 20% down. Frequently 25-30% will be needed. You'll need to have a few months of reserves in your operating account as well. Most new investors start with smaller rental buildings to build experience and equity. Prices for buildings will vary by market and neighborhood. Ex: Pueblo might have a 6-unit bldg. at $125k/door or $720k total. 20% down = $145k. Denver & Northern Co more likely @$150k/door or $900k total. 25% down = $225k.

Fix and Flips	**$125,000 and up.** 20% of the purchase price down is typical. Usually, the investor pays for the renovation work out of pocket. A "typical" estimate is based on a 20% down payment for a $400,000 property, a $5,000 reserve for purchase costs and holding costs, and $40,000 for renovation work. If you don't have this much money, you may find *hard money* loans for projects with compelling economics. Using hard money makes it MUCH harder to make a profit.
Converting Apartments to Condos	**$450,000 and up.** Realistically you will need at least 25% of the purchase price. Some renovation work is required; the investor sometimes pays for the renovation work out of pocket. Or you could get a commercial loan for 70% of the cost (LTC, loan to cost) of the purchase + renovation. A "typical" estimate is based on a 25% down payment for a $1,000,000 property (5 units for example), $25,000 reserve for purchase costs and holding costs, $25,000 to legally divide the property, and $30,000 for renovation work per door. Quickly requires more equity for larger projects. Local banks that portfolio (don't sell) their loans are the best sources.
Scrapes & New Construction	**$500,000 and up.** On land, plan to put down, in Denver, 50%. This only works in sought after neighborhoods, so expect to pay $700K - $1.2 million for the land. That's $350-600K you may need to front. Engineering, survey, design, and architecture at $50,000 or more. "Hard costs" for building a luxury home in Denver in 2024 runs nearly $300 / SF. You can probably get a construction loan for the rest. Northern Colorado won't be much less. It'd be a good idea to have some construction experience before this.

How much equity is needed will depend on where and what you buy. The starting point to understand equity requirements is the underlying price of the asset. Then, take about 60% of that for homes and condos for LTR (long term rentals). You'll want a rougher house in a rougher area to have cashflow. If you are interested in STR (short term rentals), you'll need a nicer home (or plan to renovate it) in a nicer area to make it work. These are minimum guidelines; spending more for STR will usually pay off.

Target Inv Prices	Denver	North CO	CO Springs	Pueblo
Long term Rental Home	447,000	384,000	303,000	189,000
Long term Rental Condo	282,000	264,000	198,000	162,000
Short term Rental Home	596,000	512,000	404,000	252,000
Short term Rental Condo	376,000	352,000	264,000	216,000
Income Prop / door	380,000	350,000	220,000	210,000
LTR are 60% of average price; STR are 80% of average price				

Homes and condos require 15% down; multifamily at the time of this writing needs 25% or more down.

Downpayment Needed %	Denver	North CO	CO Springs	Pueblo
Long term Rental Home	15%	15%	15%	15%
Long term Rental Condo	15%	15%	15%	15%
Short term Rental Home	15%	15%	15%	15%
Short term Rental Condo	15%	15%	15%	15%
Income Prop / door	25%	25%	25%	25%

Then we can solve for equity needed.

Cash Needed $	Denver	North CO	CO Springs	Pueblo
Long term Rental Home	67,050	57,600	45,450	28,350
Long term Rental Condo	42,300	39,600	29,700	24,300
Short term Rental Home	111,400	98,800	82,600	59,800
Short term Rental Condo	70,400	66,800	53,600	46,400
Income Prop / door	190,000	175,000	110,000	105,000
Assume STR condo are 2BR and need $14,000 furniture, furnishings + equipment				
Assume STR home are 4BR need $22,000 FF+E				
Assume Income properties are duplexes (2x doors)				

You'll want to have six months of mortgage payments in reserve in addition to these guidelines. You could get in the game with a small LTR condo in Pueblo for $25,000. A LTR home in Denver might be more like $67,000. STR will have higher cap rates (and more work, managerially), but commensurately higher returns in many cases.

Credit Score

A common misperception that new investors have is that they need to have perfect credit to invest in real estate. That is not true for all asset types – some require no credit at all, such as assignments. On the other hand, once new investors see an infomercial on TV or go to their first investing seminar, they get a perspective that they can do anything with terrible credit. That's not true either – the truth, as usual, is in the middle.

The following chart gives you an initial idea of the relative importance of your credit score with different types of investments. The following chapters will explore this in more detail. See the Chapter on the "Where the Pros Get the Money" to see how to improve your scores.

Investment Type	Minimum Credit Score Requirement
Assignments	**Terrible.** You won't use your credit score for this type of investment, which makes it open to anyone!
Rental Condo Rental Home	**Average+.** You'll be purchasing the property, usually as a non-owner occupant (since you probably already have a primary residence). The mortgage companies will look at your credit score a little more closely than they will for your primary residence. As a rule of thumb, if you can qualify (even with a high interest rate) to buy a home to live in, you will be able to qualify to buy a home to rent out. However, the interest rates will be a little higher
Small (2-4 unit) Apartment	**Average +.** The discussion for rental home and condo applies, but the standards are a little tighter when you get a slightly bigger building.
Large (5+ unit) Apartment	**Average+ / Near Perfect.** You can get a commercial loan with a credit score that is a little better than the average, but you'll pay a higher interest rate. On larger buildings, the economics are very sensitive to your financing, so if you have just above average credit, not as many buildings will make sense for you. Conversely, if you have perfect or near perfect credit, you'll be able to get the most favorable commercial rates which will increase the number of buildings that are economical to invest in. Most investors believe only the

	building matters and their credit is not considered. That is very rarely true, and never for newer investors.
Fix and Flips	**Terrible.** If you have terrible credit, you will turn to a hard money lender. They typically focus on the economics of the deal and not your credit. As a result, the number of potential investments available to you will be significantly smaller than the pool of properties available to the investor with better credit.
Converting Apartments to Condos	**Perfect.** The bank considers these to be high risk projects.
Scrapes and New Construction	**Perfect.** Very similar to "Converting Apartments to Condos."

As you can see, having terrible credit will not prevent you from getting involved in real estate investing, but it will reduce some of your choices and will make the choices you make less profitable than if you had better credit. Get started with a project and start learning, and in the meantime, take any steps you can to improve your credit scores. Make improving your credit score a permanent pursuit.

Experience with Contractors

If you enjoy improvement projects on the home that you live in now (or, at least, can tolerate them), you will probably enjoy working with contractors on your real estate projects. For many of our investors, this is a highly rewarding part of their work (at least when things are going right). Other investors find it very frustrating. To learn how to find a good contractor, refer to the Chapter on "How Successful Investors Build Their Team."

Investment Type	Importance of Experience with Contractors (or Willingness to Learn)
Assignments	**None.**
Rental Condo Rental Home Small (2-4 unit) Apt	**None / Very Limited.** Things will break in the rental units a little more often than they do at your home. But, if you overpay to get a deluxe contractor that holds your hand through every step of the process (e.g., go to Home Depot and hire their people), you are not going to significantly change the economics of your investment.
Large (5+ unit) Apartment	**1-2 Projects.** As you buy a building with more units, you are going to have to fix more things more frequently. Getting good at managing contractors will make your building more profitable. If you don't, you'll leave money on the table.
Fix and Flips	**Very Important.** Experience with contractors is what will make or break your project's profitability (and to a large extent, your enjoyment of the project, too). Even if you have at least some experiences in hiring, managing and firing contractors, this could be a great choice for you. If not, you should be willing to be actively involved to learn these skills.
Converting Apartments to Condos	**Crucial.** Don't consider this type of real estate investing until you have mastered the management of contractors. Do some small fix and flip projects first.
Scrapes and New Construction	**Crucial.** Don't consider this type of real estate investing until you have mastered the management of contractors. Do a few small fix and flip projects first.

Experience with Property Managers

This table outlines the relative importance of prior experience working with Property Managers for different types of real estate investments. As you review the chart below, you will see that extensive experience with property managers is not a requirement for any of these real estate investment types. To learn how to find a good property management company, please see the chapter on "How Successful Investors Build Their Team."

Investment Type	Importance of Experience with Property Managers (or Willingness to Learn)
Assignments	**None.**
Rental Condo Rental Home	**None / Limited.** We always advise our clients to manage their own property for at least the first year. It's an invaluable experience. If you decide to hire a property manager, you'll need to get some experience in managing them, but know that most investors for this size of rental manage the properties on their own. For most investors, it makes more economic sense to do it on their own and they learn many lessons firsthand that enable them to better select and manage property managers in the future on their larger investments.
Small (2-4 unit) Apartment	**Limited.** For many investors, this is their follow-up rental investment. They often start to experiment with delegation of at least some of the property management functions in this size property.
Large (5+ unit) Apartment	**Limited – Somewhat Important.** As your rental buildings get bigger, you'll be increasingly likely to outsource at least some of the elements of the management job.
Fix and Flips	**None.** Hopefully, you sell the property immediately after completing the renovation work.
Converting Apartments to Condos	**Limited – Somewhat Important.** Depending on the size of the building you are working in, see the discussion above. The property management elements are a bit more complex in this environment, as you may have some owners in the building alongside your tenants, with contractors improving units to the frustration of everyone. It can get a little exciting.
Scrapes and New Construction	**None.** Hopefully, you sell the property immediately after completing the renovation work.

Time Required

Some real estate investments are relatively hands-off once they are set up and running properly. Others are very hands-on. Depending on what other commitments you are trying to juggle in your life, you may not have time for a hands-on investment. This is a common source of failure for newer investors. Don't purchase an investment if you don't have the time necessary to commit to it! We segment the discussion into the number of hours to get started, then the number of recurring hours of effort each week to keep the investment working well.

Here is a rough guideline to what you can expect to get your project started. The table after that will outline your time commitments after the project is started (e.g., after you close):

Investment Type	What's required to *GET STARTED* (time you invest just once, up through and including the purchase of the property)
Assignments	**Can be extensive (60+ hours).** Usually, you will start by finding a motivated seller, then negotiating the terms. Depending on the conditions in your market this can take some time. Once you have located the property you need to find an investor to match the property. Again, depending on the market, this can also take time. Once you have located all the parties there is some paperwork to fill out on a one-time basis.
Rental Condo Rental Home Small (2-4 unit) Apartment	**40+ hours.** You will want to spend time with your real estate agent discussing your needs, then hunt for properties, then manage the closing process. Once you close, there will be some one-time setup activities (set up checking account for building, notify tenants of new landlord and payment procedure, etc.).
Large (5+ unit) Apartment	**20+ hours.** Like the smaller rental buildings but the allocation of the time is different since you have probably purchased a rental building before. It will take less time to assess your needs, and you will probably be more efficient at finding a building. However, the changeover process once you close takes longer since there are more tenants to be managed. You'll probably have a property management firm helping with at least some of the tasks, and they will need setup time (involving your input) to get up and running.
Fix and Flips	**Almost always extensive (80+ hours).** There are many steps to finding a good project, and the more time you invest up front the higher your chances for success.

Converting Apartments to Condos	**Extremely extensive (160+ hours).** Like the F&F project (and basically, this is a F&F project on steroids) there are many steps to finding a good project, and the more time you invest up front the higher your chances for success.
Scrapes and New Construction	**Almost always extensive (160+ hours).** There are many steps to finding a good project. The more time you invest up front, the better your chances for success.

Investment Type	What's required to *KEEP GOING* (time you invest every week, after you close on the purchase)
Assignments	**None.**
Rental Condo	**0 – 3 hours / week.** For the months when the property is full, you'll just have to mow the grass, shovel snow, or deal with the occasional tenant question. If you get someone on site to do the yard work, you'll have many weeks where you do nothing at all. When you have a vacancy, you'll have to run an advertisement, answer some phone calls and do some showings (again, you might hire someone to do much of this for you), but it shouldn't take too much time once you are in the rhythm of doing it.
Rental Home	
Small (2-4 unit) Apartment	
Large (5+ unit) Apartment	**0 – 20 hours / week.** If you hire a property management company, this should be closer to zero hours. If you elect to do it on your own, it still might not be much if you have a person on-site to do yard work and show vacant units for you. If you do it all yourself, it will depend on the size of the building but will generally be among the least time intensive of the real estate investments.
Fix and Flips	**Likely 10+ hours / week.** If you have extensive contractor management experience, you can get by with a lot less. If this is your first project with contractors, you'll want to be around frequently, and ideally getting your hands dirty, to build your skills and improve your chances of success.
Converting Apartments to Condos	**Likely 10+ hours / week.** Like the F&F discussion above, there will be a lot of work to do.
Scrapes and New Construction	**Likely 10+ hours / week.** If you have extensive contractor management experience, you can get by with a lot less. If this is your first project with contractors, you'll want to be

	around frequently, and ideally getting your hands dirty, to build your skills and improve your chances of success.

Number of Monthly Interactions

By interactions, we mean how often you will have to visit the property or take phone calls to answer questions. In addition to understanding the number of hours required to be successful, different investors have different preferences for the number of interactions they will need to have. Due to the balancing act of work and family, some prefer to have a smaller number of longer interactions, while others prefer many interactions of shorter duration. Which do you prefer?

Investment Type	Typical number of monthly interactions (e.g., phone calls, meetings, on-site visits)
Assignments	**None.**
Rental Condo Rental Home	**Average 1 – 5.** Should not require much ongoing effort for the months when the unit is occupied; more effort when you are filling a vacancy, less if you have management assistance. Most of the interactions will be very brief (e.g., following up on why rent is late, answering questions about a vacant unit).
Small (2-4 unit) Apartment	**Average 1 – 10.** Like "Rental Condo" above, but you will have vacancies more frequently.
Large (5+ unit) Apartment	**Average 1 – 20+.** Like "Small Apartment." If you hire out all the property management, it can be relatively easy. You'll have some longer discussions with your property manager on a monthly "status call."
Fix and Flips	**Average 10 – 20+.** If you are not experienced, you will want to check in at least several times a week with each major contractor on the team. Many of these interactions will be longer discussions (10+ minutes) as contractors explain problems that have appeared, and you discuss alternative options to resolve the issue and select the best approach. You'll probably want to be on site frequently. You might also lower your project costs by buying materials for the

	contractors and delivering them to the job site, which can be time consuming.
Converting Apartments to Condos	**Average 20+.** This is a combination of running an apartment building with a F&F at the same time; anticipate lots of phone calls. There will be plenty of longer phone calls and meetings to resolve problems, and you will work with attorneys on the HOA documents, etc. Not for the faint of heart.
Scrapes and New Construction	**Average 5 - 10.** If you hire a general contractor to oversee the project, they will be responsible for handling most of the phone calls and resolving most of the problems. If you want to be the General Contractor, then you have a new part time job.

Perception of "Hassle"

This is the toughest area to assess – what annoys one investor might be a challenging and fun puzzle to solve for the next. Look within yourself. We'll discuss how to manage some of the most common hassles later in the book. Specifically, how to select and manage contractors is covered in the chapter "How Successful Investors Build Their Team", and working with tenants is covered in the chapter "Property Management." However, there are some broad observations we can share:

Investment Type	How Much Hassle is Required
Assignments	**High – Very High.** If you don't bring a credit score or cash, you are going to have to bring your time and willingness to deal with a lot of nonsense to find a good deal. The seminars and infomercials make it sound easy, but most people find it's more hassle than it's worth. Consider yourself warned.
Rental Condo	**Very Low – Moderate.** People are people and tenants are tenants. Most are fine but some will drive you crazy. You
Rental Home	will have the occasional person that never pays on time,

Small (2-4 unit) Apartment	irritates other tenants, or is the one complaining about every possible issue. Hopefully it is the exception and not the rule. Unless you are in a dreadfully bad renter's market, keeping your building occupied usually will not be too much of a problem if you work hard and pay attention. This is not, however, a turnkey business. See the chapter on "Property Management" to learn more.
Large (5+ unit) Apartment	**Very Low – Moderate.** Most investors don't buy a larger building until they have some experience with a smaller building for a very good reason. They've already learned many lessons on tenant selection, and hopefully how to get a property manager to help them. A good property manager will make this score "very low." If you do a lot of the work yourself, you'll make more money, but you'll have more headaches, too.
Fix and Flips	**Before closing on purchase: Medium – High.** You will want to do a lot of *due diligence* (e.g., verifying all the facts that the listing agent gave you that you relied on to decide) to avoid making a mistake. This takes time. **After closing to completion of renovation: Medium** (if you have experience) **– Very High** (if you do not have experience). This can be a great way to build equity in a hurry, but it would be misleading for us to tell you that it's a walk in the park. It can be a lot of fun for the projects where everything goes well (and this does happen), but most projects will involve at least some headaches.
Converting Apartments to Condos	**Very High.** Like the "Fix and Flip" discussion above
Scrapes and New Construction	**Before closing on purchase: Medium – High.** You will want to do a lot of due diligence to avoid making a mistake…this takes time and the discipline to walk away from projects that don't make sense. **After closing to completion of renovation:** • **Medium** (if you hire a general contractor). • **Very High** (if you are the GC). This can be a great way to build equity in a hurry, but it would be misleading for us to tell you that it's a walk in the park. It can be a lot of fun for the projects where everything

| | goes well (and this does happen), but most projects will involve at least some headaches. |

Risk Tolerance

"Courage is resistance to fear, mastery of fear – not absence of fear." ~ Mark Twain

Some investors (and their spouses and/or co-investors and/or bankers) are more comfortable with risk and ambiguity than others. This chart will give you an initial orientation to the degree of risk you are accepting with different types of real estate investments.

Investment Type	Relative Degree of Risk and/or Uncertainty
Assignments	**None.**
Rental Condo	**Very Low.** This investment is relatively easy to assess, purchase, and sell if you don't like it. A small condo is probably the easiest category of rental to manage. Like all rentals, the returns are predictable and are not too volatile.
Rental Home	**Low.** Like rental condo, only you'll have to plan for outside maintenance on your own. On the other hand, you won't have HOA fees, noisy neighbors, etc.
Small (2-4 unit) Apartment	**Low.** Less risky than rental condos and homes since you have more than one unit, so it's unlikely you would ever have to make a mortgage payment completely on your own. A little riskier than a condo or rental home since it (typically) costs more to purchase and might take a little longer to sell.
Large (5+ unit) Apartment	**Low – Medium.** Less risky than other rentals insofar as the cashflow should be the most stable of any rental group. More risky than other rentals since they cost more, require more equity, and take longer to sell. In the hands of a landlord seasoned with experience from smaller buildings there's a relatively low degree of risk. Returns are certainly more predictable and controllable than the stock market.
Fix and Flips	**Medium – High.** High risk, high effort, and high potential return. Requires more due diligence up front than rental investments. Your success is largely dependent on the

	performance of your contractors who you do not directly control. Be careful. Work with pros. Consider the risks.
Converting Apartments to Condos	**High / High+.** All the factors for an apartment building and a Fix and Flip.
Scrapes and New Construction	**High.** High risk, high effort, and high potential return. Just like Fix and Flips, and then some.

Which Investing Category is Best for Your Unique Situation?

Follow the ten questions to determine which real estate investing categories are best suited for your unique situation. Take your time – the better you reflect on this now, the fewer mistakes you will make later.

Question 1: Do you have average or better credit? We will explore credit scores in exhaustive detail in the chapter "Where the Pros Get the Money."

- If your credit score is below 620, you have poor credit.
- If your score is above 660 assume you have average credit.
- If your score is above 720, assume you have excellent credit.

If your score is above 660, the answer is yes, proceed to question 5. If not (your score is below 660), go on to question 2.

Question 2: Can you make an investment of at least $25K? If the answer is no, go to question 3. If yes, go to question 4.

Question 3: In this case, you currently do not have a strong credit score and you are limited to the funds that you can invest. Do you enjoy (or at least are willing to try) working with contractors?

- If you are not willing to work with contractors, you should consider Assignments.
  - This will get you started while you rebuild your credit and save up a downpayment.
- If you are willing to work with contractors, you can consider a consider a fix and flip project.
  - You will need to get a Hard Money loan that finances both acquisition and repair costs.
  - You need almost 100% financing. That is rare; you'll need an exceptional deal, which will take a lot of time to find.
  - Since the project funding will be tight, you will probably have to do a lot of the work yourself.

- o   However, this could be a good method for you to build your equity reserves in a hurry if your marketplace currently has a good market for F&F.
- o   This is a high intensity sweat equity project!

Question 4: Do you have a lot of time on an ongoing basis to allocate to your real estate investing interests?

If you do not have a lot of ongoing time, then you should consider getting a small rental property. With your current cash resources and credit score, you will most likely want to choose a rental condo; a rental home is likely out of your budget.

- You could get a 1BR condo rental for $100K or less in Pueblo, CO, so your cash investment could be at/under $25K.
- The cheapest 1BR rental condos in Denver are closer to $200K, so you'd need closer to $50K in cash for down payment and perhaps another $10K in reserves.
- You can adjust this for the market prices in your target market.

As you build equity in a few years, you can refinance your property and you will have more capital to deploy. Also focus on building your credit score, and this will serve to increase the options that are available to you.

If you do have a lot of ongoing time to invest, you have more choices. You can choose to pick a smaller rental as outlined above, or if you like working with contractors (or have the desire to learn), you could work on a small fix and flip.

- If you choose a F&F, you will likely need to get a Hard Money loan that finances the acquisition costs and the repair costs.
- Since the project funding will be tight you will probably have to do a lot of the work yourself.
- However, this could be a good method for you to build your equity reserves in a hurry if your marketplace currently has a good market for F&F.

Question 5: We have established that you have at least an average credit score. Do you have at least $70,000 to invest? If not, please jump to question 9. If you do have at least $70,000 you would like to invest, continue with question 6.

Question 6: Are you willing to take on at least a moderate level of risk to get higher returns? If yes, and you want to focus on the higher risk opportunities to earn higher returns, please skip to question 8. If you want to start with less risky investments and are accepting lower returns, continue to question 7.

Question 7: We have established you have a good credit score, at least $40,000 to invest, but you want to limit your risk. Do you have a lot of time to invest with your real estate investments on an ongoing basis?

If you do not have much time, then a rental strategy is probably best for you.

- If this is your first time as a landlord, you'll want to start small.
- You can afford a condo, home, or small apartment building.
- Condos and homes require less money, but they have more cashflow volatility (e.g., if the tenant moves out you make all the mortgage payment).
- Slightly larger buildings will require a little more money, but the cashflow is more dependable (if one of the four tenants moves out, the other three tenants will pay most or all the mortgage for you).

If you have some experience as a landlord, you should consider a larger (more than five unit) building.

- With your experience, this will also be a low-risk investment, and with a competent property manager it won't take too much of your time either.
- In any case, you will probably want to purchase a building without a lot of risks (e.g., not many vacancies, in a nice part of town, and/or not much deferred maintenance) to reduce your exposure.

Question 8: We have established you have a good credit score, at least $70,000 to invest, and you are willing to accept more risk to get more return. Are you experienced working with contractors?

If you are not experienced but are willing to learn, a fix and flip project would work.

- You will not have the constraints that a Hard Money lender will often apply to applicants with less credit power.
- You will have the financial freedom to hire contractors to do the work and not have to do most of the work yourself.
- If it is your first F&F project, start with something simple even if you can take on more risk. Don't be a hero to start!
- Once you have had a successful project, move on to more complex projects. Walk before you run, and you won't be a statistic!

If you are experienced with contractors, you should consider whether an apartment conversion (if the market cycle is right) or a scrape and new construction is right for you. This is the highest risk category, but it also can have the highest returns and affords considerable tax planning flexibility that the other investment choices do not offer.

If you have strong credit, ample cash, and willingness to take on risk, but you don't want to deal with contractors, your best choice may be to buy a rental building. (We will explore the difficulties of working with contractors later in the book).

- If you don't have much property management experience (either first-hand or managing the managers), buy a less ambitious project (e.g., a "retail" building), learn about how to manage a building, and then in the future, consider a more difficult project (e.g., a "distressed" building).
- If you do have property management experience, you could consider buying a distressed building that is being sold below market. Many rental investors do not have deep property management skills, so you won't be competing with as many people for the investment, thus you can often get a better

price. Examples of factors that cause distress are high vacancy rates, significantly deferred maintenance, and/or weak property management (often manifested as below-market rents). Since buildings usually sell as a multiple of cashflow, you can buy the under-performing building at an attractive price, fix the issues causing distress, then re-sell the building at a higher price. This is a great strategy if you have the time and inclination to do it!

Question 9: You have at least an average credit score, but you have less than $70,000 available. Do you enjoy working with contractors? Or are you willing to try?

- If not, proceed to question 10.
- If you are willing to work with contractors, you should consider a fix and flip project.
    o You will not have the constraints that a Hard Money lender will often apply to applicants with less credit power, and you will have the financial freedom to hire contractors to do the work.
    o If it is your first F&F project, start with something simple even if you are willing to take on more risk.
    o Once you have had a successful project, move on to more complex projects.

Question 10: You have at least an average credit score, you have less than $70,000 to work with and you don't want to duke it out with your contractor every Friday afternoon. Do you have a lot of time, on an ongoing basis, to allocate to your real estate investments?

If you do not have a lot of ongoing time, then you should consider getting a small rental property.

- With your current cash resources, you will most likely want to choose a rental condo, a smaller rental home or a small (2- 4 unit) building.
- As you build equity in a few years, you can refinance your property, and you will have more capital to deploy.

If you do have a lot of ongoing time to invest, you have more choices.

- You can choose to pick a rental as outlined above.
- You could choose to pursue a lease option strategy. That doesn't work well in this market, but it might be an option in the future.

Summary. This chapter requires a great deal of self-analysis, a discipline which does not come naturally to many of us. We suggest you return to the beginning of the chapter and walk through the flowchart on the last page again…slowly and deliberately…with someone you trust. It's critical you spend the time to get this right. Otherwise, you risk pursuing the wrong type of real estate investment and severely reducing your chance of success.

If you and your family are honest, none of these active paths might be a good match. If that is the case, passive real estate investing is likely the path to take.

And if Ironton Capital can be of service to you to make your journey easier, let's talk about how our passive funds could fit into your portfolio at https://irontoncapital.com/gopassive

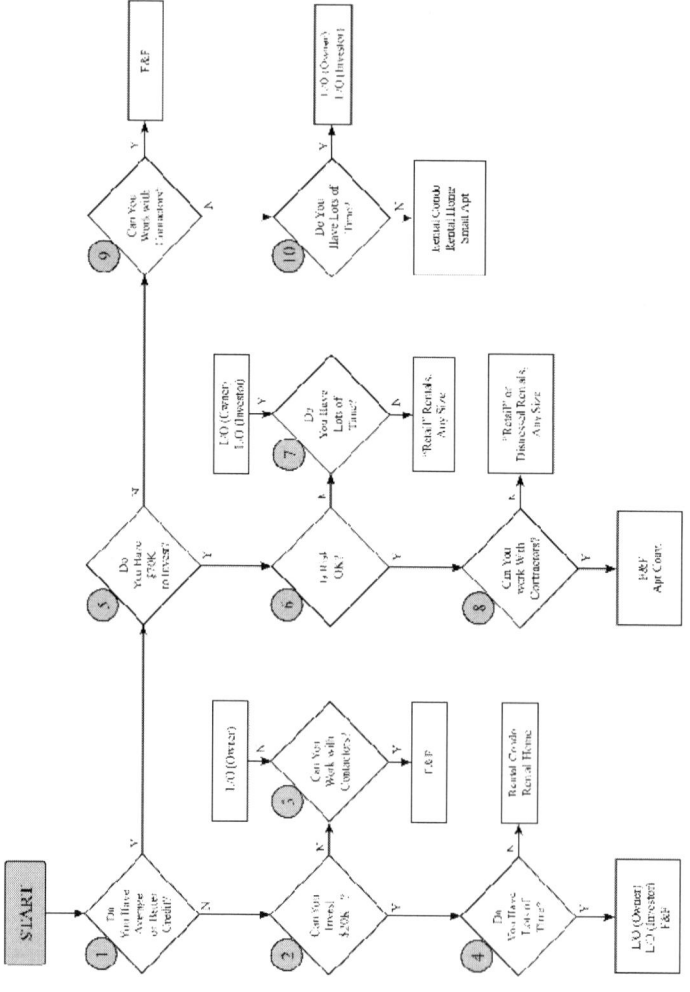

Made in the USA
Middletown, DE
13 July 2024